BOAT BUILDING IN WOOD

BOAT BUILDING IN WOOD

From Lofting to Launching

Colin Faggetter

WATERLINE

Published by Waterline Books
an imprint of Airlife Publishing Ltd
101 Longden Rd, Shrewsbury, England

ISBN 1 85310 530 9

A Sheerstrake production.

A CIP catalogue record of this book
is available from the British Library

Typeset by Servis Filmsetting Ltd
Printed and bound in Great Britain by
Butler and Tanner Ltd, Frome and London

To all those yachtsmen who aspire to build their own boat

At long last we are afloat, but still lots to do.

Contents

BOAT BUILDING IN WOOD

Enjoying the fruits of his labours.

Introduction

There is nothing quite like building a boat to stir the imagination and bring out the best of our endeavours. It is a labour of love for the builder, to see the craft grow from a pile of timber to something that has beauty and life.

The work involved is neither difficult nor hard, but just enough to tax your ingenuity and resolve, with a result that is very rewarding. The ultimate moment is on the day when she slides into the water amid champagne and applause and when one soon forgets all the seemingly difficult problems encountered during the building.

It is to address those problems that this book is written. I hope through these pages to take some of the mystery out of boat building, by taking the reader through the entire procedure from lofting to launching. This book is therefore for the novice who is building his or her first boat and requires to learn something of the techniques used, however mundane they would appear to someone who has already 'done it'.

I feel that the best way to explain things is to actually build a boat and for the purpose of this exercise I will use two of my own designs, a double-chine Goosander 27 and then complement it with a round bilge Goosander 25, thus covering both types of hull construction.

The interior construction will of course be similar but using different techniques, as will be described later.

The construction methods as detailed in this book will apply closely to other similar designs, and I hope will give the reader an overall picture of the procedure and technique used. My own boat, which will be used as the subject, is a Goosander 27, modified from the drawings used here and built some ten years ago.

Five years ago I sailed *Goosander* to Greece where it is now moored at Palaia Epidavros. Now that I am retired I am able to make good use of it. My pleasure can be summed up in one phrase – 'Enjoying the fruits of my labours'. I would hope that reading this book will allow other amateur builders to do the same.

It must be stressed here that building a boat is not in any way a short-term project, but something in the order of five years or more steady work. This is a somewhat arbitrary figure as the time factor will be related to the time available, equipment and ability, nevertheless it seems to be a reliable average.

It is best not to have, or even think of having any pre-conceived dates of completion – they are seldom met. But don't be put off, it is always worth it in the end and all the head scratching is soon forgotten.

Goosander *on her mooring in Greece.*

Chapter 1
Plans and Choice of Boat

There are several companies that advertise in the yachting press and who supply boat plans that range from simple dinghies to large ocean-going craft, both power and sail. These plans are usually very detailed and include timber lists and some will supply full-size patterns for the frames. In fact the wide choice offered can be bewildering at first sight.

Most potential builders will however, have a fairly good idea in their own mind of the type of craft they are looking for. If the following questions can be addressed, then a suitable design near to your ideal will almost certainly be found.

What type and size of boat do you want to build? Single or double-chine, round-bilge, long-keel or fin-keel, bilge-keels or centreboard, Bermudan or ketch-rigged and how many berths do you want? Where will you be sailing and how far, estuary or further afield? How much money is available initially and thereafter over a period of say five years?

Trying to advise a potential amateur builder that 'this' is the right boat for him, will almost certainly end up with a clash of ideas. Individuals have their own ideas, not only on the external appearance but also on the layout of accommodation and interior. There are so many possible permutations that only tentative advice can be offered.

I remember when at Fox's yard in Ipswich, we built a Goosander 23 as a demonstration vessel and thereafter built hulls and produced kits for home completion. During this time I spoke to over three hundred and fifty potential customers, all amateurs enquiring about the various stages of completion. The most interested, and some of those we felt needed a little more persuasion, were invited for a demonstration sail. Some were enthusiastic, others had reservations on all conceivable things. Could they move the galley two inches forward? Could they have three inches more head-room? Could they raise the sheer by four inches? Why was the quarter-berth so narrow? Could they move the bulkhead three

inches aft so as to increase the berth to six and a half feet? These and many more questions and suggestions provided much food for thought.

My own plans obviously reflect how I see my ideal, but in the end the amateur can, within reason, incorporate his own ideas within the hull, provided that the engine, fuel and water tanks are not moved to any extent, which in a small boat may upset the trim, which in turn could well effect its sailing performance.

One thing that became clear to me at that time was that almost everyone wanted to put too much into a given hull volume. There is a common pre-conception that all boats should have a separate toilet compartment, a shower, chart table, a fully-fitted galley and voluminous locker space. All this is possible in a thirty-two foot length boat but if you are contemplating something at around twenty feet these ideas will need modification. However, with a certain amount of ingenuity it is surprising how much can be achieved. In a small boat it is advisable to keep the layout simple and practical.

The plans that are eventually purchased will hopefully be close to your requirements and with careful consideration some of your own ideas can be incorporated, bearing in mind certain accepted parameters such as the minimum measurements for berths etc.

It is generally agreed that a single or double-chine hull is easier and quicker to build than the round-bilge variety. Some will not find the single or double-chine hull pleasing to the eye, but this shortcoming can be mitigated by careful design of the chines, the ends and subtle use of the angles used. This is more easily achieved in the double-chine hull.

I have endeavoured to produce drawings that should clarify the methods and techniques explained in the text.

Chapter 2

Lofting Chine Hulls

When the plans arrive amid great excitement, they should be studied long and carefully from border to border. This will give an overall picture of all aspects of the construction and how the drawings relate to each other in one way and another. Hopefully there will be a timber cutting list, so that these items can be ordered and made up while the lines are being lofted. Unless you are fortunate enough to have a good timber merchant nearby, one who can supply all your requirements, it is advisable to seek a specialist. There are several who advertise in the yachting press who will be able to supply species of wood not usually stocked by the general merchants.

Most of the wood for my boat was bought from a local timber yard. This was at a time when there was a surplus of elm. I purchased a sixteen by two foot diameter log of wych elm and had it cut into boards of various thickness and also two lengths of five by six inch for the deadwood. This was then put in-stick under cover and left for two and a half years to season. It is normal to consider one year per inch of thickness for seasoning. What about the deadwood sections? Well they proved to be reasonably dry even after this short period, however it was another two years before it was eventually painted. For the remainder of my wood I had to go elsewhere.

Lofting is to draw out the design lines to full size on a suitable floor area. The object being to correct any inaccuracies in the offset table and to facilitate making up the frames and templates for the deadwood, horn timber, floors and stem etc. A good flat area is required on which to lay down sheets of ply. Cheap 6mm fir ply is quite suitable and in the case of the example in Fig 1, eleven or twelve sheets would be more than adequate and with a bit of juggling could be reduced to ten. They should, if necessary be fixed to the floor and lay flat. The joins should then be taped with wide masking tape and the whole given a couple of coats of white emulsion.

Equipment
The equipment required for lofting is as follows:

Two long wooden battens (approx 1 × ⅝in and ¾ × ½in and at least 18ft long) preferably made from spruce, Douglas fir or British Columbian pine. The main criteria here is to be straight grained and knot free, so that they will bend in a uniform curve.

One perspex batten (approx ¾ × ¼in and 6ft long) of good quality and very flexible so as to allow it to take up fairly tight curves. Also useful is a similar batten of ⅝ × ⅛in for really tight curves.

Light hammer & Pincers

1½in steel pins

Masking tape

Coloured fine felt-tipped pens & H grade pencil

Rubber

Tracing film

Pricker

Steel measuring tapes – 3m and 10m lengths.

Builders string-line

Wooden straight-edge (3m length)

Tick-sticks (white plastic are best)

Large square (3 × 3ft) cut from lofting material

Large pair of compasses, useful for drawing in station lines geometrically.

Small kneeling-cushion

The lines for a chine hull are relatively simple as also is the grid. A thorough study should be made noting the relationship of the offset table and the various lines that it refers to. It should be noted that in the example, the half-breadth plan will have to be closed up to the profile by about twelve inches to accommodate the lofting boards, assuming you have laid them horizontally and used three in the vertical (ie making twelve feet).

It should be ascertained from the offset table, which line is being used as a reference for the vertical offsets. It will either be a base line or as in Fig 1, the waterline.

This should now be struck in at an appropriate position using the builder's line. The line should be as tight as possible and about ¼in above the surface of the boards. This will allow a series of tick marks to be made directly beneath the line, later to be joined with a straight-edge. The base line and half-breadth centre-line can now be added in the same fashion, making sure that they are parallel. These lines should now be sighted by eye to confirm that they are indeed straight. If not they must be corrected.

The station lines can now be drawn, starting at 'B'. The measurements between the station lines should be added up in aggregate and noted. Referring to Fig 1, they should read 2ft 9in, 5ft, 7ft 3in, 9ft 6in, 11ft 9in etc to 25ft 3in, 27ft. A tape can now be hooked over a pin at 'B' and these measurements marked off accurately along the base line. This method is superior to using individual measurements, which can lead to progressive error.

It must be stressed that the 'grid' must be as accurate as possible and every care must be taken to ensure this. All these points should be numbered as shown.

Vertical station lines can now be erected both above and below the base line. This can either be done using the square with the straight-edge on the base line, or if you have a large pair of compasses, using the geometrical method, learned many years ago at school (See Fig 1b). These lines can now be extended to the length required. It is sensible, having completed the station lines, to measure the intervals at top and bottom to ensure accuracy. We can now start on the lofting proper. It is best to start with the lines that will not be

changed later. These are the sheer in profile and half-breadth, stem face, rabbet and transom in profile. We can now take from the offset tables the relevant measurements of these.

Starting with the stem in profile, go to the first column in the tables marked 'sheer'. We find at 'B' the vertical measurement of 3ft 3⅜in, '0' being 2ft 11in and station 1 being 2ft 8⅝in etc. All these points are marked on the appropriate stations. These points can now be 'pinned' and a long batten offered up from below and then held in place with additional pins. The batten should be allowed to pass the top of the stem by a couple of feet to aid any further fairing in the vicinity of the stem. The batten can now be sighted by eye for any hard spots, if there are any, the pin near or causing the hard spot should be removed. If you have got it right, the batten will spring a fraction and should present a good fair line. However you may find that it is not a hard spot but a flat spot, in which case the batten will have to be pushed and held by an additional pin or two.

It is unlikely that you will have a full length batten, so most of these lines will require two 'goes', so to speak. The thing here is to remember to retain some of the pins and slide the batten along. In doing so you will create a continuous fair curve. It is also worth noting that when penciling in the line, the batten should be firmly held down since it can easily be distorted when pressing the pencil against it. Having practised with the sheer profile, the remainder of the profile can be lofted including the chines, transom and keel. Then comes the half-breadth plan including the keel half-breadths, and the chines. The waterline can here be left out.

An explanation of the keel half-breadths may not go amiss. It will be seen that the keel, stem and horn timber are shown in a continuous line. The horn timber, starting at the transom is 3in wide, this measurement is continued along to the sternpost. Coming back up to the top of the keel/deadwood, it starts to increase in width at 1ft 4in aft of station 8 until at station 7 it is 5in wide. This continues right up to the top of the stem. Going back down the stem it can be seen that the stem face is 1in wide until station 1 and thereafter widens out to merge with the ballast keel.

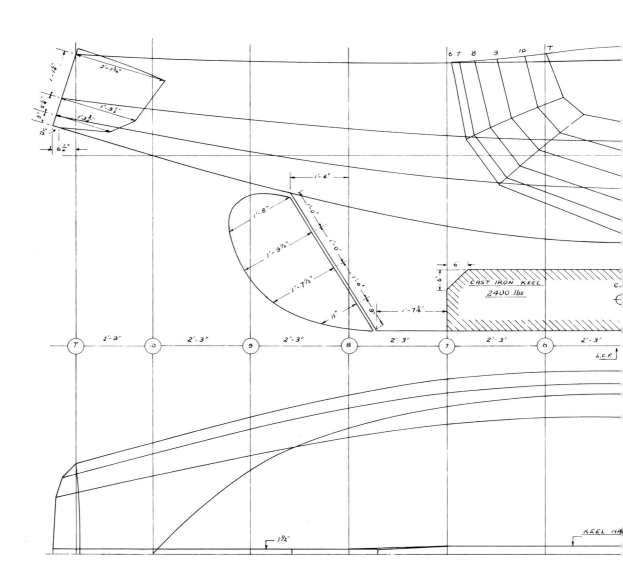

Fig 1 *Line Drawing of Goosander 27*

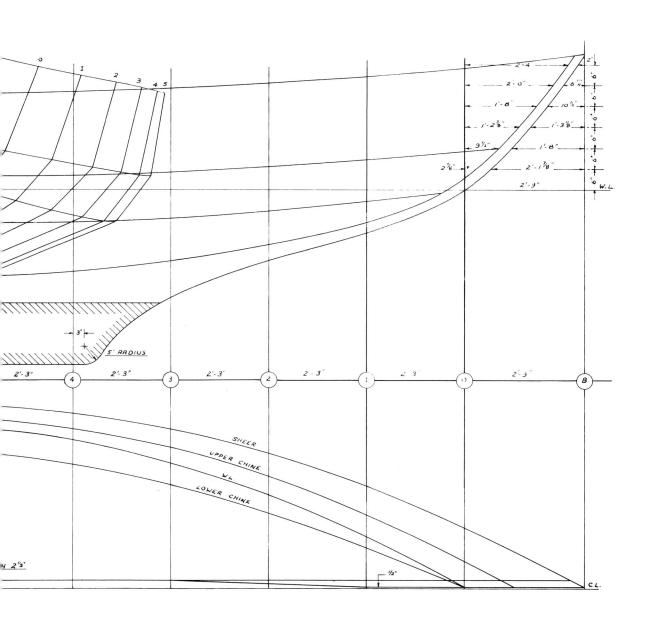

	HEIGHTS ABOVE AND BELOW WATERLINE						HALF BREADTHS			
	Sheer	Upper Chine	Lower Chine	Rabbet	Keel Bottom		Sheer	Upper Chine	Lower Chine	Rabbet
B	3-3-3	1-0-4	0-0-0			O	1-5-5	0-7-7		0-2-6
O	2-11-0	0-11-0	0-0-0	0-3-4		1	2-6-0	1-3-6	0-11-5	0-3-0
1	2-8-3	0-8-5	0-3-3	0-9-5	1-0-5	2	3-3-6	2-8-2	1-9-4	0-2-4
2	2-6-3	0-6-6	0-6-1	1-3-7	1-8-5	3	3-10-2	3-4-2	2-5-5	0-2-4
3	2-5-0	0-5-0	0-8-0	1-8-3	2-7-3	4	4-2-1	3-9-5	2-11-6	0-2-4
4	2-4-0	0-3-7	0-9-2	1-11-5	4-3-0	5	4-4-0	4-0-2	3-2-5	0-2-4
5	2-3-4	0-3-4	0-9-3	2-1-2	4-3-0	6	4-4-2	4-0-3	3-3-1	0-2-4
6	2-3-1	0-4-2	0-8-4	2-0-0	4-3-0	7	4-2-1	3-10-1	3-1-2	0-2-4
7	2-3-0	0-5-6	0-6-4	1-8-4	4-3-0	8	3-9-3	3-5-6	2-9-4	0-2-0
8	2-3-1	0-7-7	0-3-2	1-2-6	3-1-6	9	3-3-3	2-11-5	2-4-3	0-1-4
9	2-3-4	0-10-4	0-0-7	0-7-5		10	2-8-1	2-4-4	1-10-1	0-1-4
10	2-4-1	1-1-5	0-5-4	0-0-2		T	2-1-6	1-9-4	1-3-6	0-1-4
T	2-5-1	1-4-4	0-11-5	0-8-7						

Offsets for Goosander 27 (Feet, inches and eighths)

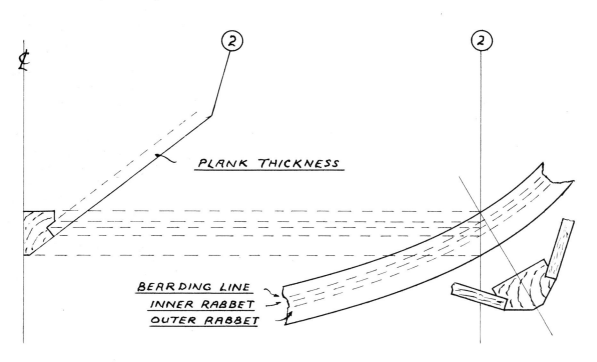

PLANK THICKNESS

BEARDING LINE
INNER RABBET
OUTER RABBET

Fig 1a *Projection from stem to body-plan at station 2*

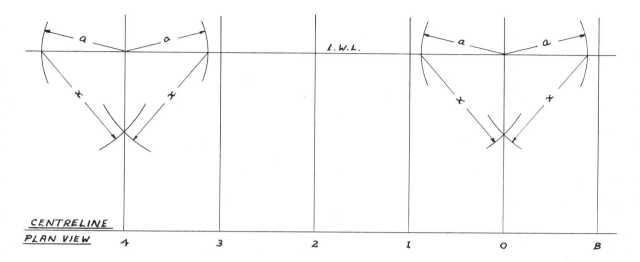

CENTRELINE

PLAN VIEW   4   3   2   1   O   B

Fig 1b *Finding the vertical for station lines by use of compass*

Now on to the body-plan from which the floors, frames and hog sections can be deduced. The body-plan is drawn up using station 5 as the centre-line. The stem and keel widths should be drawn in. It will be noted that the keel width on the right hand side is parallel from keel bottom to top of stem, the left side tapers in at station 7 to a point parallel to the top of the sternpost and thereafter is 1½in wide. Similarly there is a taper on the other side from station 3 to station 1. It now remains to transfer horizontally the heights at sheer, upper chine, lower chine and rabbet at each station, combined with the half-breadths. On the drawing-board this would be done with a tee square and dividers. As this is impracticable we can turn to the tick-stick. Fig 3 shows how the tick-stick is used. Using the waterline and centre-line as datum, the horizontal and vertical measurements thus found can be penciled in very lightly and the intersections joined by bolder lines. It is as well to remove these light lines to avoid possible confusion later. As far as the right side of the body-plan is concerned, it would be better to use station 4 for trans-

ferring the vertical points, still using the waterline as datum and the waterline for half-breadths, using the centre-line as datum. This will keep the measurements near the centre of the half-body-plan and will help eliminate potential inaccuracies. For the left side, station 6, the waterline, and the centre-line.

Having drawn in all the frames, it is only left now to run-in the sheer and chines. As seen in Fig 1, these are a gentle curve, with a slight upturn between stations 4 and 5. This is to be expected and due to the closeness of these frames as represented by the drawing. The transom can now be drawn in as shown, using dimensions from the lofted half-breadth plan. The inner rabbet line and the top of the hog can now be drawn in, the actual thickness of the material being used for the hog must be used here. It is now possible to draw in the hog sections on the body-plan, taking the width from the half-breadth plan together with the hog thickness. The plank thickness should be drawn in completely on each body section.

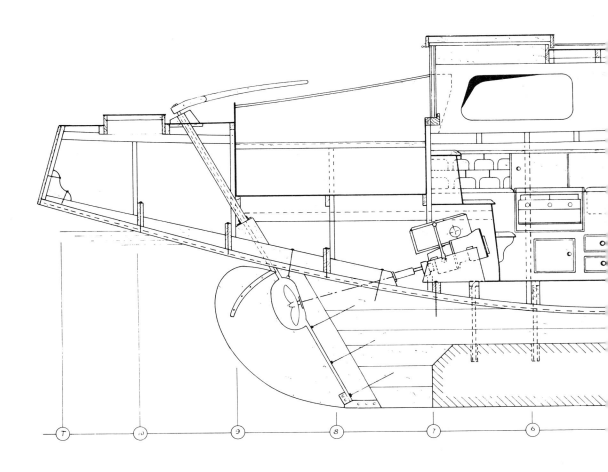

Fig 2 *Goosander 27 general construction plan.*

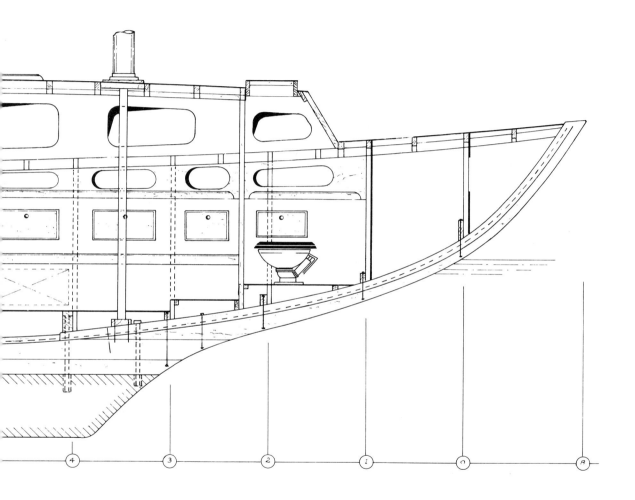

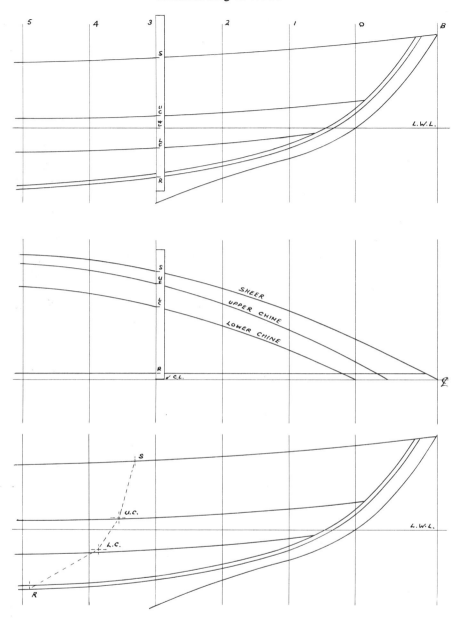

Fig 3 *Using the tick-stick*

Things now tend to get a bit messy, so it is better to use a coloured felt-tip pen for this stage of the proceedings. To add further to the confusion the floors can now be added, the height being taken from the construction drawing as shown in Fig 2. These should be drawn in using a different coloured pen. It will be noted that the floors at stations 8, 9 and 10 straddle the horn timber. These floors can be drawn in as solid, the notches being cut out when they are being made up. The only two remaining things to do are the rudder profile and ballast keel, both being quite straight-forward.

Chapter 3

Lofting Round-bilge Hulls

I am using the lines of Goosander 25 to demonstrate the lofting of round-bilge hulls. You will notice at a first glance that it is looks a lot more complicated than for a chine hull. But since you have digested the previous chapter I have no doubt that you will be familiar with the basic procedure!

As with the chine drawings, the accuracy of the 'grid' is all-important; otherwise it will be difficult, if not impossible to fair-in the lines. To save space, and therefore lofting boards, the keel and curve of areas can be left out and the half-breadth plan closed-up to the profile. The profile must again be drawn in to show sheer, transom, keel

bottom and stem – and on the half-breadth plan, the sheer.

We now run in and fair the waterlines. Fig 4 shows the method used to locate the ends of the waterlines on the centre-line. This also applies to the aft end. In practice, the transfer of these points should be made from a convenient station line, by tape, dividers or tick-sticks, the latter two methods being the most accurate. It will be noted that the curves of the waterlines aft of station 6 are tight, so this is where the perspex batten comes into its own. As mentioned in the previous chapter, a good overlap of the batten should be used to create a continuous fair line.

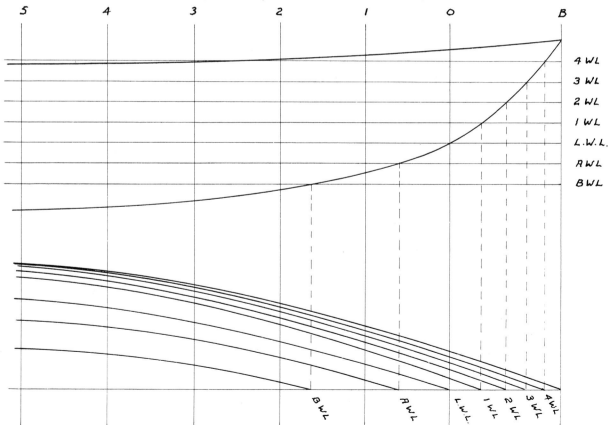

Fig 4 *Transferring waterlines onto half-breadth plan. (Not to scale)*

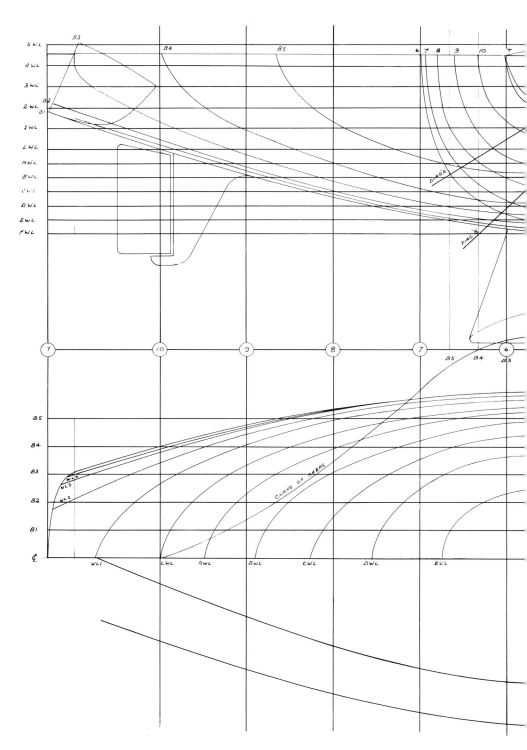

Fig 5 *Line plans of the Goosander 25 to demonstrate a round-bilge hull*

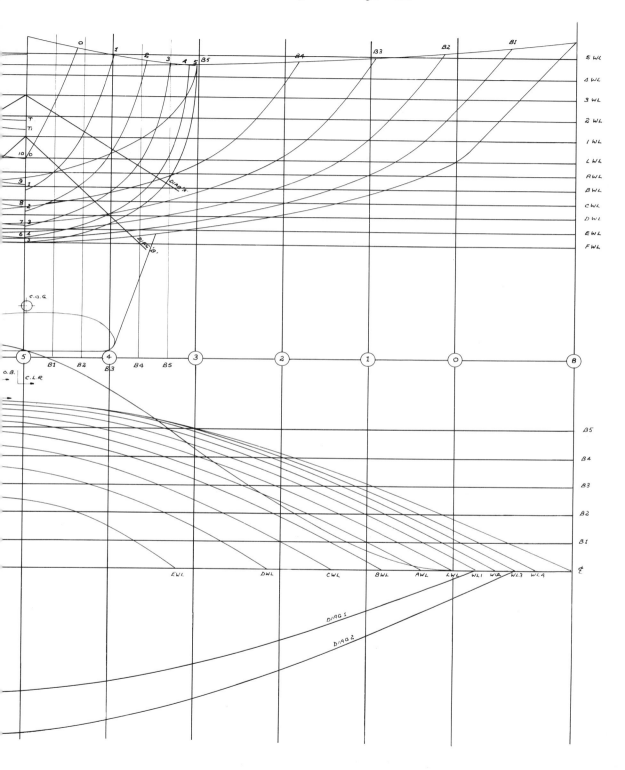

Buttock Lines

Now for the buttock lines. The offsets for these will be found in the top section of the offset tables (Fig 6a). Observe that the figures enclosed within the box are measured from, and are below the waterline. A short description of buttock lines and their function will not go amiss here and will help you to understand what you are actually doing.

Buttock lines represent a vertical slice through the hull, parallel to the fore and aft centre-line and therefore shows the shape of the hull at that slice. As in the case of the example, five buttock lines have been used. (Fig 5)

Buttock lines, waterlines and the body-plan all have a relationship and should correspond on the three-dimensional view. In this instance, an illustration can replace a thousand words and Figure 6 shows how these points are transferred and how they are all related. Use tick-sticks or dividers and the nearest station or waterline as datum.

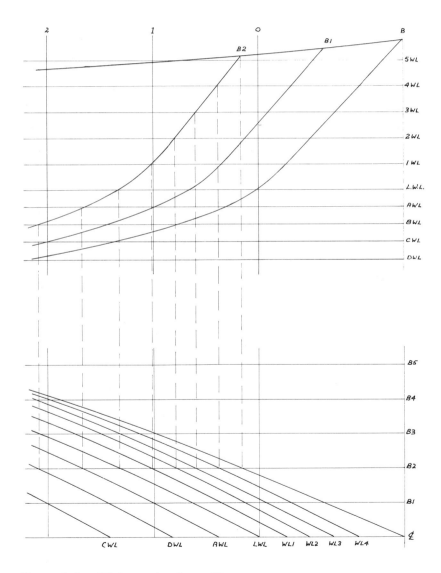

Fig 6 *Projection of buttock line B2 from plan to profile*

STN	DIAGS B	DIAGS A	HOG/STEM	SHEER (HB)	WL 4	3	2	1	L.W.L.	A.W.L.	B.W.L.	C.W.L.	D.W.L.	E.W.L.	HOG	KEEL BOTTOM	1	2	3	4	BUT 5	SHEER (HT)
B			0-2-0	0-0-0																		2-11-0
0	0-3-0	0-8-3	0-2-0	1-2-4	0-11-4	0-8-7	0-6-2	0-3-4	0-0-0						0-5-2	0-0-0						2-6-6
1	1-0-7	1-7-2	0-2-0	2-0-3	1-10-4	1-8-4	1-6-3	1-3-5	1-0-3	0-7-8	0-2-3				0-9-4	0-3-7						2-5-5
2	1-8-4	2-4-6	0-2-6	2-8-7	2-7-7	2-6-6	2-4-6	2-2-3	1-11-1	1-7-2	1-2-7	0-7-7			1-0-6	0-7-3						2-4-2
3	2-2-6	3-0-5	0-4-0	3-3-7	3-3-5	3-3-0	3-1-3	2-11-2	2-8-3	2-4-7	2-1-4	1-7-5	0-11-7		1-4-6	0-9-2	0-1-0					2-3-2
4	2-8-1	3-7-1	0-5-0	3-8-7	3-8-7	3-8-5	3-7-2	3-5-4	3-3-1	2-9-2	2-4-7	1-10-1	1-0-2		1-7-0	1-0-5	0-2-5					2-2-6
5	2-10-6	3-10-3	0-5-0	3-11-1	3-11-1	3-11-1	3-10-2	3-8-7	3-6-7	3-2-0	2-10-2	2-3-7	1-7-3		1-9-7	1-6-0	0-5-5					2-2-5
6	2-10-0	3-10-6	0-5-0	3-11-4	3-11-4	3-11-1	3-10-4	3-9-1	3-6-7	3-2-5	2-10-5	2-4-7	1-6-4		1-8-4	1-0-6	0-2-6					2-2-6
7	2-6-6	3-7-3	0-4-4	3-9-7	3-9-7	3-9-7	3-8-6	3-7-3	3-4-4	3-2-2	2-9-5	2-4-3	1-7-7		1-4-5	0-11-0	0-2-0					2-3-0
8	2-0-1	3-2-5	0-3-7	3-6-6	3-6-5	3-6-3	3-5-2	3-3-4	2-11-5	2-7-3	2-0-5	0-11-7			1-0-6	0-3-6	0-9-0	0-3-6	0-7-7			2-3-1
9	1-5-2	2-8-4	0-3-4	3-2-2	3-1-5	3-0-7	2-11-4	2-8-4	2-2-5	1-6-4					0-5-0	0-7-2	0-6-2	0-5-1	0-1-5	0-5-3		2-3-2
10	0-7-7	1-11-4	0-2-7	2-7-7	2-7-1	2-6-1	2-3-2	2-0-5							0-0-0	1-9-1	2-7-7	2-6-1	0-2-4	0-0-0	0-1-2	2-3-3
T.		1-2-7		2-0-5	1-11-6	1-10-3	1-5-0								0-4-7	0-8-0	0-8-6	0-10-7				
T		1-0-3	0-2-0												0-10-5							

Fig 6a Offsets table (feet, inches and eighths)

Body-plan

At this point, be assured that you are not reading a sex manual – we move from buttocks to body! In fact the body-plan. To speed up the process of transferring the half-breadths at the waterline you will find that the tick-stick comes into its own. As a first step, the height of the keel bottom as at station lines should be transferred to the centre-line of the body-plan at station 5 together with the top of the stem. These points must be clearly numbered , as should all waterlines and buttocks, each

end. This helps to follow the lines by eye a great deal easier.

Figure 7 illustrates the use of the tick-stick and uses station 4 as an example. The stick should butt onto the centre-line as shown and each waterline accurately ticked together with its designation. To maintain the correct orientation of these marks the stick should be used forward of station lines 0 to 5 and aft on stations 6 to 10. The stick can now be butted onto the centre-line of the body-plan and the sheer half-breadth ticked in.

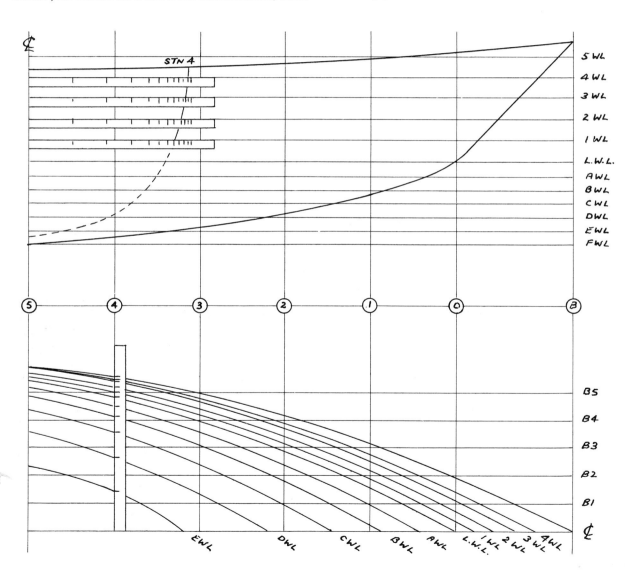

Fig 7 *Method for using the tick-stick*

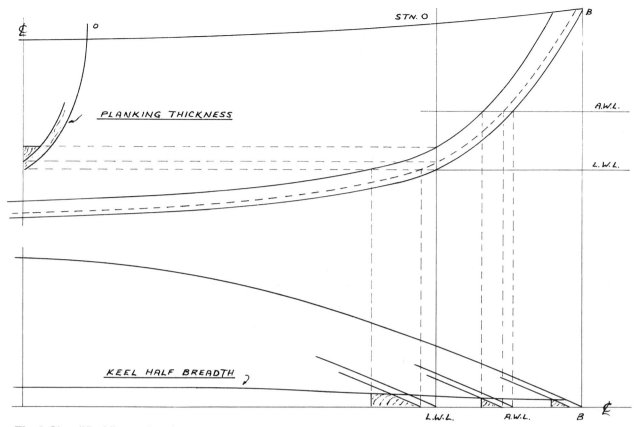

Fig 8 *Simplified lines showing cross-section (Not to scale)*

This, combined with the height of the sheer at station 4 will establish the first reference point. The stick is now moved down to WL4 and so-on until EWL. All these points can now be pinned and faired-in using the perspex batten. If all appears correct, clean the batten and proceed to the next frame. If however there is a kink, or you see something odd, solve the problem before moving on. Never leave anything 'to be sorted-out later' – it will prove very much more difficult to solve and may well upset other lines as you continue.

The body-plan can now be completed. A further check can be made on the fairness of the body-plan by using the diagonals 'A' and 'B' shown on the lines drawing. Note where these lines start and finish so that they can be drawn in accurately. The offsets for these are found at the bottom of the table in Figure 6a.

We can now move on to show the cross-sections of the stem, hog and the planking deducted on the body-plan. Figure 8 should clarify this step but note that all unwanted lines have been deleted. The width of the hog and stem sections are shown in the half-breadth plan. Also shown dotted on the profile is the bottom and actual face of the stem, together with the inside face of the hog and stem. The outside line of the stem is known as the ghost line, which is in fact the finished outline of the hull when planked.

When taking off the planking thickness on the body-plan it is best to use a short block of wood of a width equal to the planking thickness. Dimensions perhaps 1¼in long, ¼in thick and 1in wide, equalling the planking thickness. This is best drawn as a pecked line with a felt-tip pen, so that when tracing-off prior to making up the moulds, the wrong lines are not picked up by mistake. We shall return to the lines in a later chapter.

Chapter 4

Making Templates

There are many elements in the construction of a boat that require a template to be made and there are several different methods of making them. Some are quite complex and rather tedious and others are wasteful in the use of material, leaving little that can be used again. The pieces you pick for a template are often likely to be too small — Murphy's Law at its best!

The method that I favour and is also used by most professional boat builders is extremely accurate, quick and economical on the use of materials. The only tools required are a hand stapler taking 5mm or 6mm staples, a pair of tin snips, a hefty pair of scissors and a staple-puller.

The material required is a sheet of 3mm ply made of either mahogany or birch and cut into 1in strips running with the grain, Birch ply is fairly hard and is therefore more suitable if an air-operated staple-gun is available. The great advantage of the following method is that intricate and quite large templates can be made up accurately and quickly. In Figure 9 I have shown a few examples of the way in which these templates can be used and that curved templates present no problems.

A good example is where a shelf is required in a locker that has been cleated around. Two pieces are stapled together to form the correct length of each side (See Fig 9). These are single stapled to the cleating to hold them in place. The front batten is now stapled into place. If the shelf runs out to the hull, then the method shown in Figure 9 is adopted. The two holding staples can now be removed and the template carefully lifted out. It sometimes happens that the template can only be removed by distorting it. This should be taken as an indication that you will probably not be able to get the shelf in, unless perhaps it is made of 6mm ply which can be manipulated fairly easily. If it does prove impossible, then the shelf must be made in two pieces and fitted 'dry'. If the fit is satisfactory, one piece can be removed, then edge-glued and replaced with perhaps a couple of wedges to close up the glue line.

When making the templates, it is essential to reach right into the corners to ensure that a true shape is found. When marking round any template where there are straight sides, it is only necessary to mark round the corners and join with a straight edge. When creating a curved side there will be a series of small peaks and flats as shown in Figure 9. A series of tick-marks should be made and then faired in with a batten to produce a smooth curve.

The other type of template is the semi free-standing type also shown in Figure 9. This is best started on the frame, going round the chines or webs. The horizontal and vertical members should be put in using a spirit level and the whole suitably braced. Due to the angle of the chines it may be difficult to remove, an alternative method is shown in Figure 9. With a little practise these slight aberrations should cause few problems. After laying the template on the ply and tracing around, the finished shape can be drawn in.

When stapling free-standing templates and where there is nothing solid to staple against, a solid object must be used, a hammer head for instance or the two pieces held firmly together with a pair of pliers. This will help prevent bounce, if however the staple is not fully home then the pliers can be used to press the staple home. I normally put two staples into each joint. There is nothing worse than having prised the template away, to carry it to the bench only to find several joints then fall apart. After a little practise you will find it quite easy. Once the template has been used it can be dismantled so the pieces can be used again.

Having laid the template on the material and penciled around, it should be noted if any edges require a bevel and in which direction. This must be allowed for when cutting-out. Square edges can be cut to the line, allowing just a whisker to be faired off with a plane.

There are other methods where hardboard, stiff paper or thin ply can be used. A solid template comes into its own when used to lay out jigs for something such as a laminated stem or deck

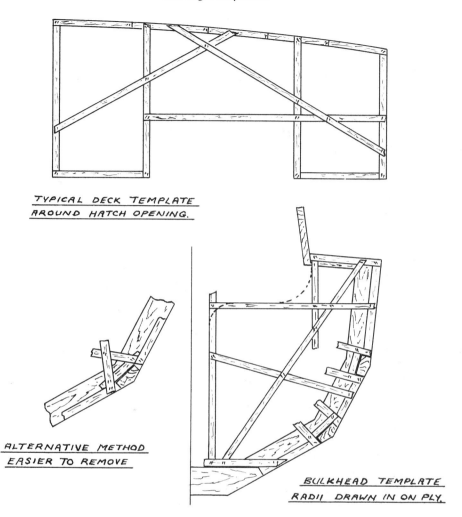

TYPICAL DECK TEMPLATE
AROUND HATCH OPENING.

ALTERNATIVE METHOD
EASIER TO REMOVE

BULKHEAD TEMPLATE
RADII DRAWN IN ON PLY.

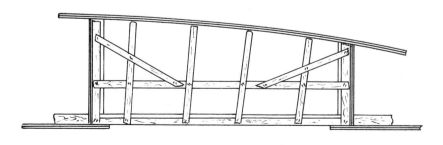

LOCKER SHELF.

Fig 9 Templates

beams. Also for the shape of the deadwood, sternpost, horn timber etc. In this instance a tracing can be made on the lofting of the horn timber for example, together with the station lines and other reference points. This tracing can then be pricked through onto the template material, faired in and accurately cut to the line. Finally to be laid on to the timber or hardboard and drawn around ready for cutting out. On this type of template, which may well be used in conjunction with another, all station lines and other relevant lines should be drawn.

A word of caution
After a certain amount of use you will find that you have battens of all lengths. They should be hidden away when not in use. They are migratory by nature. We found in our workshop that our stock of short battens was always depleted, probably because they make ideal paint stirrers!

Chapter 5

Timber, Ply, Fastenings, Glue, Epoxy and the Tools Required

We have all seen those advertisements which say 'Build this dinghy in two week-ends – the only tools required are a screwdriver and a hammer'. Maybe, if the wood is pre-cut and pre-drilled. Building a boat from scratch is a different matter altogether and a reasonable selection of tools is essential, plus as much equipment as can be afforded. By equipment I mean a planer, saw-bench, and/or a band-saw and an open table bench for cutting ply (See Fig 10). This can be made quite quickly and cheaply out of sawn 4 × 2in, and by laying a ⅝in sheet of Douglas fir ply on top it becomes a most useful bench.

Someone contemplating building a boat may well be of a practical nature and already possess a reasonable selection of tools. The following list is a good basic guide but as different jobs arise it will be found that owning the right tool for the job makes the task much easier, and also will help produce a better end result.

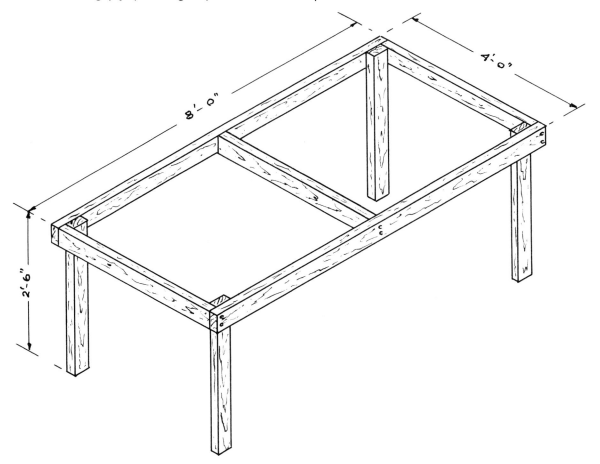

Fig 10 Simple ply-cutting table constructed with 4 × 2in sawn timber

Basic Tools

Light hammer
Heavy hammer
Steel plane
Rebate plane
Spokeshave
Spokeshave, round
3m steel tape
10m steel tape
Handsaw
Tenon-saw
Keyhole-saw
Oil stone
Plumb bob
Combination square with spirit-level
3ft spirit level
Bevel (sliding type)
Set of wood chisels ¼in to 1in (6mm to 25mm)
Set of hole cutters
Pair of adjustable steel dividers
Hand drill with a full set of twist drills
Spade bits for electric drill ¼in to 1in (6mm to 25mm)
Stanley countersink bits Nos 6, 8, 10 and 12
Set of plug cutters Nos 6, 8, 10 and 12
G cramps 3in, 4in and 6in. (You cannot have too many)
2 × 3ft sash cramps
A good strong workbench with vice.

Electric Tools

6in saw-bench, perhaps combined with plane
Electric hand plane
⅜in electric drill
¼in cordless drill (very useful)
Jigsaw (the best you can afford). This is the most essential and versatile tool you will use. My own preference is the electric, variable-speed Bosch which I have used for many years – it is virtually indestructible.
Router. A useful addition that will help to provide that professional finish.
Orbital sander

Plywood

Plywood, whether marine or otherwise is supplied in sheets measuring 244cm × 122cm and in thicknesses of 3.5mm, 6mm, 9mm, 12mm, 19mm and 25mm. This provides an ample choice to work with.

It is wise to use only ply that conforms to BS1088 (or appropriate national standard) in which both the quality and number of veneers together with the adhesive used is strictly controlled. Ply that is sometimes sold as 'marine ply' but doesn't show the BS1088 stamp or kite-mark should be treated with caution for use on the hull or deck but may well be considered for use on internal structures such as lockers and partitions. Good marine ply is not cheap. Bruynzeel give a twenty year guarantee on their ply – well worth considering.

For internal use, and where a decorative finish is required there is a choice of different veneers on either one or both sides. Most common are teak, sapele, ash, oak and birch, all of which provide an attractive contrast.

Adhesives

From the many types available, it is often best to stick with the one you find easiest to use and prefer. All the following are waterproof and have a long life.

Cascamite™

A urea formaldehyde resin that takes the form of a white powder and is mixed with water to a creamy consistency. You only mix enough for the job on hand. Pot-life is reasonable and the product can be purchased in most hardware shops. It is most suited to internal joinery work and is clean to work with. It will not stand total immersion in water.

Aerolite 306™

This is a synthetic resin and also comes in powder form which is mixed with water to the consistency of syrup. A catalyst in the form of ascetic acid is used. The resin is applied to one surface and the catalyst to the other. As long as the timber remains damp the glue will cure. I have found that the best method to apply the catalyst is to use a spray, directed to the resin. Keep this product away from your hands as it tends to burn (which only becomes apparent a few days later).

This type of glue is gap filling and good for all boat work. The resin, if kept in an airtight container, will remain usable for two or three months. If it becomes too thick, a little added water will usually restore it to its correct consistency. Aerolite is highly water resistant, heat resistant and immune to attack by mould or fungi.

Cascophen Resorcinol Resin – 2 Part
An extremely durable waterproof adhesive for gluing wood that will withstand complete exposure to the elements. It is easy to mix and apply.

Epoxy Resins
There are several established manufacturers of epoxy resins. For the purpose of this book the following descriptions concern Structural Polymer Systems Ltd.

SP106 Wood/Epoxy System™
A general purpose epoxy system for use on a wide variety of materials including GRP, steel, aluminium and concrete. It is supplied as a two-part resin and is available with fast (SP209) or slow (SP207) cure hardener to suit different working conditions. As a coating, it is used to protect and strengthen wood.

Filling and Fairing
When modified with filler powder (SP106) this system provides an ideal surface preparation for subsequent coatings. As an adhesive it creates a high-strength, low-shrinkage joint combined with high gap-filling properties.

SP Fillers
SP Colloidal Silica™
Extremely fine particles of silica serve to thicken a liquid epoxy system. The change in handling properties can be varied from a slight increase in viscosity to resist sag or drainage, to a thick gap-filling paste. Always added in combination with other fillers.

SP Glass Bubbles™
Hollow white glass spheres, similar to microballoons, but higher in density which when added to the adhesive produce sanded light-weight filler mixes.

SP Microfibres™
These are fine, white, milled wood-pulp fibres that can be added to the adhesive to prevent drainage from glue joints. They will also produce gap-filling and fillet bonding mixtures. To aid accuracy in the mixing process, it is advisable to buy the mini-pumps which screw onto the container. This will provide the required volume ratio.

Mastics
There are many mastics on the market. For our purpose a few products of 'Boatlife' will be described.

One-part Life-Caulk™
For deck caulking, seaming, sealing fittings and bedding hatches and portlights. This can be used on damp surfaces or even applied under water in an emergency. Moisture helps the curing process. Curing time is approximately ten days depending on the conditions.

Two-part Life-Caulk™
Surfaces here must be dry and curing time is around forty-eight hours. Good for laid decks and can be sanded or painted.

Liquid Life-Caulk™
A thinner version of the one-part Life-Calk. Good for sealing problem areas.

Marine Silicon Rubber
This is a one-part marine grade silicone rubber but is not intended for continuous underwater use. The cartridges here will require an open barrel caulking gun.

This is but a brief description, a saunter around a chandlery will reveal all you need to know about this subject.

Lets take a wry look at mastic. It is I think, the most insidious material invented by man. With the greatest will in the world, it is impossible to stop its migration to every conceivable part of the hull, deck or workshop. Once it leaves the tube, there is no hope. However careful and methodical you are, you cannot win.

The classic case is the rubbing strake. Having cut the nozzle at the correct angle and aperture and loaded it into your calking gun, you proceed to run a couple of beads along its full length. Then it is out with the putty knife to spread it nice and evenly. By the time you are approaching the end you are beginning to get a good surplus building up on the knife. You must now look for a piece of scrap ply to scrape it on to. With a flair for forward-thinking you will have laid out all the screws along the deck, thrown a couple of rags up, a screw-driver and just in case – the mastic. Here you will need a helper. The rubbing strake can now be laid onto the scaffold planks while you jump up, then lifted into place at the stem, while your helper holds it up with arms at full stretch eagerly awaiting your instructions.

Having managed to drive the first screw in, its 'Up a bit', 'In a bit', 'Sorry, down a bit'. All this is of course depositing a nice ridge of mastic on the deck-edge and several inches down the hull. You are now collecting mastic on your screwdriver, which will steadily work its way up the handle. If you have not collected any mastic on your sleeve, don't worry, this won't be long now. After having used your rag a few times for wiping your hands and screwdriver and other sundry places, it will begin to deposit mastic wherever you drop it. You will also have noticed that the gun has exuded mastic on the deck, did you forget to release the trigger?

By now of course your helper's arms are begin-ning to wilt and your urgent call for 'Up a bit' do not seem to have that immediate response, hence more mastic on the hull. By now your helper has also forgotten how to hold the rubbing strake by the top and bottom edge and has wrapped his fingers right around it, smearing mastic along several feet in the process. His big problem is, that he does not know how to tell you, although you will find out soon enough.

The job is now nearing the end and at last your helper can leap up onto the trestle and align the last few feet for you. It will not have been noticed until you have time to relax that your shoes try to defy gravity. The answer is simple, you have mastic embedded in the soles. Those few blobs that dropped onto the scaffolding went totally unnoticed while you were feverishly pumping in screws. And to think, you have the other side to do, plus two toe-rails! Being a practical person you will arrange things differently next time. It will make not the slightest difference, all you can do is just press on.

It is probably best at this stage to leave the mastic to cure and deal with it later by scraping it off. Truly a story of gloom and doom. You have been warned!

Fastenings

It is important for the boatbuilder to use the proper fastenings appropriate to the job in hand. Boats operate in a harsh environment and the corrosive forces of salt-water.

Underwater fastenings must be salt-water resistant, whereas above water some relaxation can be allowed. For underwater use, bronze, A4 stainless-steel, silicon-bronze and galvanised iron are ideal. Above water all of these three plus brass, chrome, plated brass and aluminium are in order.

Brass screws

These are the most commonly used screws on boats above water and for internal fittings. If the hull is to be sheathed they could also be used underwater. Only buy the best quality, they will have a slight sheen on them. Some brands appear very bright and these have a high zinc content which eventually leaches out and leaves the screws with little strength – they also tend to sheer more easily when being driven home.

Stainless-steel screws

These are reasonably priced and it is worth con-sidering their use everywhere. There are two basic grades, A2 for above water and A4 for below water. A4 is of course the more expensive.

Silicon-bronze screws

Fairly expensive and are best used underwater. They are made in all gauges and up to 6in in length.

Silicon-bronze Gripfast nails

These nails can be used anywhere aboard and come in lengths from ⅝in to 3in, countersunk or flat head and 8, 10, 12, 14 and 16 gauge. In the thinner sizes it is not necessary to drill a pilot hole. In the larger sizes drill a pilot hole half the diameter of the nail. These nails are supplied in boxes by the kilo for 14 and 16 gauge. If you happen to bend one with a hammer, pull it out and use a fresh one.

Chrome-plated brass screws

These can be bought as countersunk, raised head or roundhead and are mainly used for fastenings with a decorative appearance, such as window frames, instruments and other internal fittings. These types of head are also available on plain brass and stainless-steel screws.

Coach screws

These are normally galvanised mild steel and can be hexagon or square headed. They come in a variety of diameters and lengths up to about 12in. The pitch of the thread is fairly coarse and they take a good grip. They are useful for fastening medium sized timbers such as floors, horn timber, knees and where a through fastening is not practical. Sometimes difficult to find galvanised – a good builder's merchant or specialist ironmonger is the best bet.

Galvanised nails

These are cheap and effective and take a really firm grip. Provided that they are adequately protected there is no great problem in using them.

Coach bolts

These are made in a variety of diameters, with lengths up to about 14in. They are dome-headed with about ¼in of squared shank below the head. This ensures that when tightened, they do not turn. Use them to secure engine-beds, stem scarfs and in fact anything that requires through-bolting. At the stem, the head can be ground down to form a 'T'. When drilling for these bolts, the hole must provide an interference fit.

Machine screws

These can be brass, bronze or stainless-steel, countersunk, raised-head or round-head and are threaded for their full length. They are particularly useful for deck fittings where different thickness pads are being used, or where one fastening goes through a deck beam and its opposite number through the deck and pad. You will not find yourself running out of thread! If you use normal part-threaded bolts you should measure for all the different lengths and diameters required to make sure you do not run out of thread.

Dumps and drift bolts

Rarely used these days except for barge work. They are lengths of galvanised rod, slightly tapered and rounded at one end and used like coach screws to hold the deadwood, sternpost or horn timber together. The hole to be drilled for dumps should be ¹⁄₁₆in undersize so that they can take a firm grip. A seven pound hammer is required here.

All fastenings are helped with a smear of light grease or even water can help. If grease is used, it must be wiped away from the timber with an acetone solvent.

Timber

Type	Weight lbs/cu/ft	Durability
Aframosia	44	Good
Ash	44	Poor
Birch	42	Poor
Cedar(red)	25	Very good
Douglas Fir	33	Moderate
Elm (English)	35	Good if completely wet or dry
Elm (Wych)	43	Good if completely wet or dry
Elm (Rock)	51	Good if completely wet or dry
Iroko	41	Very good
Larch	37	Good
Mahogany (Brazilian)	32	Good
Oak (English)	47	Good
Oak (Japanese)	45	Good
Pine (Parana)	35	Poor
Pine (Pitch)	41	Very good
Pine (British Colombia)	35	Moderate
Redwood	32	Moderate
Spruce (Sitka)	28	Moderate
Teak	42	Excellent
Utile (African)	40	Good

Note
If the moderate or poor timbers are treated with preservative, their lives can be considerably enhanced.

Chapter 6

General Construction and Setting Up

At this stage, your timber requirements should be to hand and also perhaps the ballast keel.

Keel

The plans may indicate which foundry can supply a keel for your particular boat. If however this information is not forthcoming, then a pattern must be made. This can be made from the keel drawing (Fig11a). The pattern can be made up solid or by using a combination of ply and timber as shown in Figure 11b. It should be noted that cast-iron shrinks on cooling by approximately ⅛in per foot. The keel in the example is 8ft 9in long, so the pattern should have an overall length of 8ft 10⅛in and a depth of 1ft 6¼in. The shrinkage in the width will be minimal and can safely be disregarded for all practical purposes. It is not necessary to indicate the position of the keel bolts or studs on the pattern. The dimensional plans of the keel as shown in Figure 11a should accompany the pattern so that the foundry can drill and tap the correct centres for the holes. The foundry may also be able to manufacture keel bolts, the lengths being taken from the lofting and bearing in mind that the heads will be flush with the floors. The lengths of the bolts are always measured from the underside of the heads.

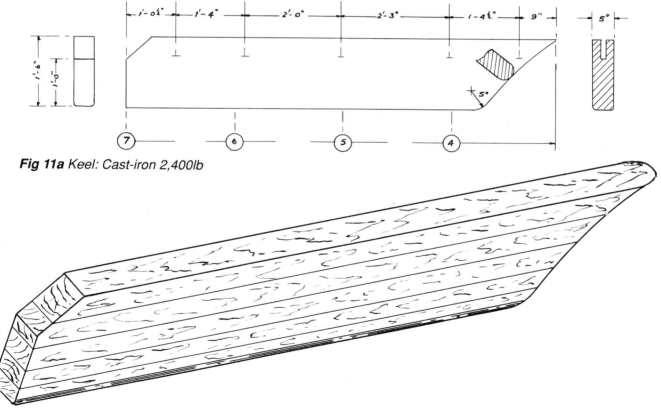

Fig 11a *Keel: Cast-iron 2,400lb*

Fig 11b *Laminated keel pattern*

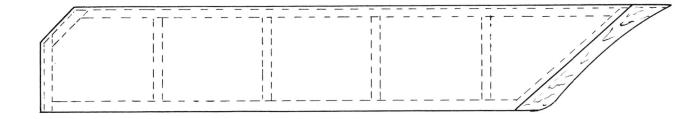

Fig 11c Hollow keel pattern – ply on frame

Which way up?
Many chine boats are built upside-down (your plans may recommend this), but I prefer to build right-way-up. This method does not require a building frame or a turn-over of the finished hull. It also means that the keel can be fitted at an early stage and used as a datum from day one. You will however discover in a later chapter that round-bilge hulls are best built upside-down. If you wish to build inverted, then use the principles as for round-bilge construction. The difference is that the frames are permanent, whereas the moulds used in round-bilge hulls are removed once suitable bracing has been fitted and are only put there as a means of producing the correct shape.

Templates
Templates can now be made direct from the lofting for all the parts required to set up the 'back-bone'. These comprise the stem, all deadwood, sternpost and horn timber. You will also need a template representing the top of the keel that shows the bolt holes. (The purpose here is to reproduce any anomalies in alignment.) Full-sized holes should be drilled in the template, which can be used later on the underside of the dead-wood as a drilling guide. Now produce the templates for the transom and framing, making an allowance for the planking thickness and the bevels.

Make the templates and show both station and rabbet lines (Fig 12). These can be laid on the lofting to be checked for accuracy. When you are happy that all measurements concur you may proceed to make the various parts shaped in both profile and plan. The plan shape should also be applied from the lofting to the finished parts. If the keel is completed, make a template of its aft end (Fig 12) to check that it conforms to the deadwood templates.

Stem and deadwood
The stem can be sawn from solid wood or it may be laminated. If it is sawn it should be scarfed.

Lamination
Laminating is easier and a jig can be set up to the outside of the stem template as in Figure 13a. A sheet of ¾in Douglas Fir shuttering ply is suitable. Wood blocks screwed from below can be used, but as they must be fairly substantial in dimension, they will use much of your G-cramp stock. This situation can be remedied by cutting out a number of ply cramps and wedges as demonstrated in Figure 13b. Remember to allow for the thickness of the lamination utilized and also the size of the wedges required.

An alternative is to make up a number of brackets as in Figure 13c, with two holes in the base, drilled for either No10 or 12 screws. Ply cramps can still be used, combined with G-cramps. I suggest that the angle irons are set at no greater than 7in or 8in centres. This ensures that the lamination is pulled down well. If any slight gaps do appear, apply a few cramps and wedges.

It is essential to lay polythene sheet on the jig and to extend it to the top of the jig angles. This will contain the excess glue that exudes and keep the jig clean – more importantly, it will also stop the lamination gluing itself to the base-board. If felt desirable, small blocks of wood can be placed on top of the polythene and although they may

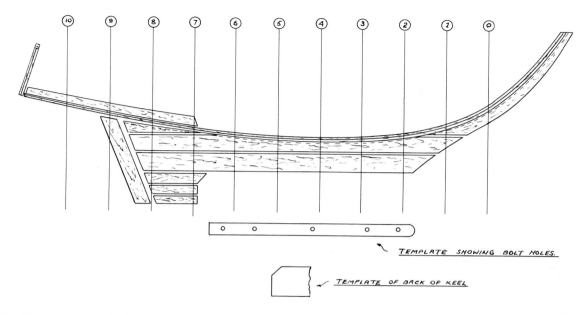

Fig 12 Arrangement of templates for deadwood and stem

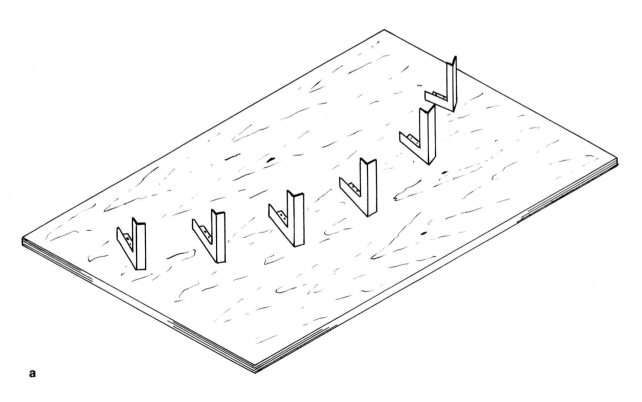

a

Fig 13a Laminating board

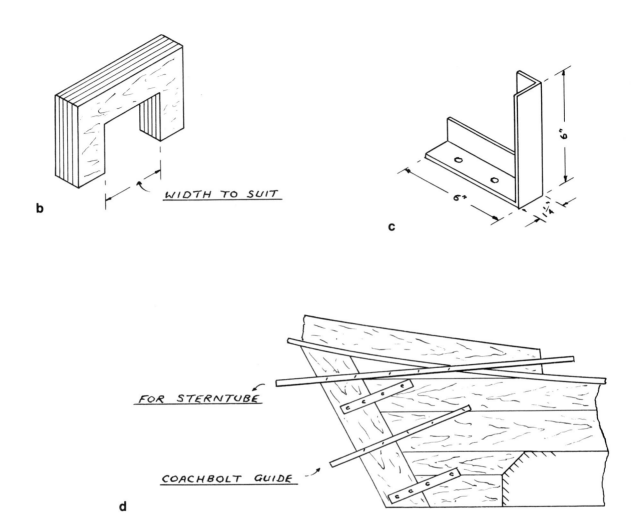

b

WIDTH TO SUIT

c

6"

6"

FOR STERNTUBE

COACHBOLT GUIDE

d

Figs 13b, c and d

stick to the lamination, they can be removed by a sharp hammer blow. When it comes to the stem, where perhaps eight ½in laminations are used, it is advisable to take it in two steps. This creates less strain on the jig and since there are only four laminations instead of eight you will benefit from a shorter 'closing' time. Before the cramps are finally tightened up, the laminations should be hammered down using a block of wood. When all is level they can be tightened. But do check again.

The entire deadwood and the stem can now be glued together on strong trestles, rather than the keel. The aft end of the deadwood being cramped together with a sash-cramp on either side.

Sternpost

Now for the sternpost. This is glued and bolted with ½in by 14in long, galvanised hexagon-headed bolts. The sternpost must be securely fastened by temporary battens screwed on to either side of the deadwood as shown in Figure 13d. This will hold it firmly in place while being drilled for the fastenings. Staple a light batten on the side to act as a guide and draw a centre-line on the aft face of the sternpost. A countersink hole should first be drilled for the screw heads. Now use the appropriate extended bit to drill a hole at least 1in longer than the bolt. By measuring in as shown in Figure 13d, a 1in hole can be drilled in at the side of the deadwood to link up. The bolt can now be inserted and if everything works to plan, the nut started and jammed with a screwdriver, and the head of the nut used to tighten up. When all three bolt holes have been drilled, the bolts and sternpost can be removed, then glued and finally bolted tight. This may sound hazardous but if the job is not rushed it should work well.

There are also two other methods of fastening the sternpost. These utilize either galvanised drift bolts or coach screws. The former is a rod with a mushroom-head and with a slightly tapered rounded end. These rely solely on friction for their grip so the hole should be drilled $\frac{1}{16}$in undersize and the drift hammered home with a lump hammer (They can be tight). Coach screws are probably the easiest to use and should be drilled for as screws, and with a washer under the head they will pull up really tight. It is advantageous to arrange these fastenings so that they penetrate at least two layers of deadwood to tie themselves together.

Hog

The hog can now be fashioned. Do as much work on the bench as is possible. Scarfs should be made before any shaping takes place, and the apron, say from station 2 to the top of the stem is best laminated. This can be done either on a jig or on the inside of the stem itself. As there would only be two laminations, no undue strain would be imposed on the stem. Make an allowance for the length of the scarf where it joins the hog after removal and cleaning up.

An easier alternative is to butt the two sections. Draw a centre-line on the hog together with station lines. As far as the apron is concerned, the station lines must be drawn on at the laminating stage, having been transferred from the lofting itself.

Mark in the half-breadth at the station lines and

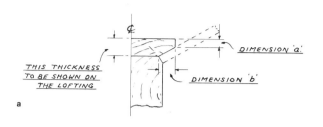

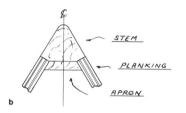

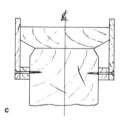

Fig 14 a, b and c

join them with a fair line before sawing to shape.

Referring to the body-plan and Figure 14, it will be seen that both dimensions a and b can be applied to the hog and apron at the station lines — these points joined and the bevel planed on. Leave a little for the final fairing prior to planking. The bevel on the deadwood and stem which receives the edge of the planking should be applied before fastening the hog and apron. This ensures a fair and even face throughout. It will become apparent that the bevel changes slightly and more rapidly towards and then at the stem. Here it is advisable to create only an approximate bevel, also as with the apron, and then correct this once the frames have been erected and a batten run through.

The hog and apron can now be glued and fastened. Use either screws or galvanised nails. You may well need a helper to make sure that the hog is running true and not running off as you fasten it. For the single-handed I suggest the idea shown in Figure 14c which should keep things true.

Observe that on the general construction drawing (Fig 2), that the hog will be left to overhang and can only be fastened when the horn timber is in place. This can now be fastened, taking particular care with fastenings between stations 7 and 8 in the vicinity of the sterntube – use cleating as in Figure 15a here. This cleating can be fastened to the horn timber first and pre-drilled for screwing into the hog. Referring to Figure 15b, the ply cover strip should be fastened when fairing for the planking is complete.

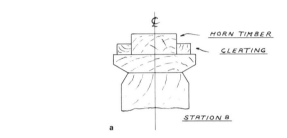

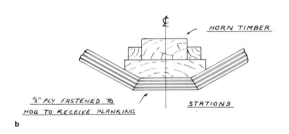

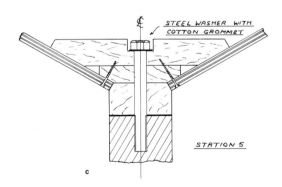

Fig 15 a, b and c

Floors

All the floors can now be made up. These should be clearly shown on the body-plan and also on the profile which also shows the amount of bevel to be applied. It is best to trace the half-floors together with the centre-line. This can then be pricked through onto the floor material and turned over to complete the full shape. Figure 15c shows a typical section at station 5 and the two screws holding the floor in place, while the keel bolt is drilled out.

All the other floors should be glued and bolted with galvanise coach bolts. Where there is a sole, the floors should be countersunk as for the keel bolts. Make sure that all the floors are perfectly square to the centre-line, otherwise you will be unable to square up the frames.

Keel bolts

You will need help to turn the back-bone onto its side. It needs to be well supported to prevent any undue strain. Using the top of the keel template, the bolt hole centres are transferred to the underside of the deadwood. It is as well to transfer the template onto the top of the floors, not only to check that the floors will line up with the holes, but also for drilling down, so halving the potential error. A batten, which will have to be packed out, is now stapled on to the side of the deadwood with one edge representing the centre of the bolt, and with a helper to guide you in the horizontal plane, a pilot hole is drilled. If you are satisfied that all is going well, carry on. alternatively, stop halfway and drill down from the top. Any slight error at this stage can be corrected when using the final drill bit, which should be $\frac{1}{16}$in or $\frac{3}{32}$in oversize so as to allow a little leeway to jiggle the bolt in.

The electric drill used for this operation and also later, the sterntube, must be fairly slow running. The other alternative is a hand auger. This of course does not allow for a pilot hole to be drilled first, but I prefer the auger despite the fact that it is fairly hard work and slow compared to the twist drill. The cost of purchase is quite modest and it requires no modification. The only thing needed in addition is a handle. A suitable diameter piece of dowel is ideal. In order to keep the auger working well and therefore pulling, it is

necessary to withdraw it frequently to clear the hole of shavings and to keep the threads clear. You soon realise when this needs to be done as all progress stops and pushing harder makes no difference.

Setting Up the Backbone and Keel

The keel can now be set up vertically and level. The top of the keel should have a straight edge run over it and any lumps and bumps ground down. It should be set up just off the ground and secured in a cradle as shown in Figure 16. The cradle can be constructed by using 4 × 2in sawn timber. Check that all the threads in the keel are clean and well greased. Try all the bolts to confirm that they start easily and run down to their full depth.

Before coating the top and aft end of the keel with mastic, carry out a dry run. Place a couple of 2in blocks of wood on top of the keel and lower the backbone onto them. The bolts can then be dropped through and any discrepancy will be seen immediately. If all is well, remove the backbone to apply the mastic and proceed to tighten down the bolts. It is advisable to give them another 'tweak' after a week or two, to really fully tighten them.

Transom

The transom can now be fitted to complete the backbone. Plumb-lines are now dropped from the top of the stem and the transom. By sighting from both ends, any slight twisting can be seen and rectified by shoring. In any case the transom must be shored up from the floor to keep it plumb. Continuous sighting and checking at all stages of building is essential and any mistakes can be spotted at an early stage and rectified before it becomes more difficult, very difficult or even impossible.

Making Up Frames

All the frames can now be made up. The planking thickness must be drawn in on the body-plan, preferably in colour to help avoid mistakes. Although this method is slightly arbitrary, it is quite good enough for practical purposes. If drawn in on the body-plan it can be seen that the true plank thickness to be taken at station 1 is $\frac{3}{16}$in

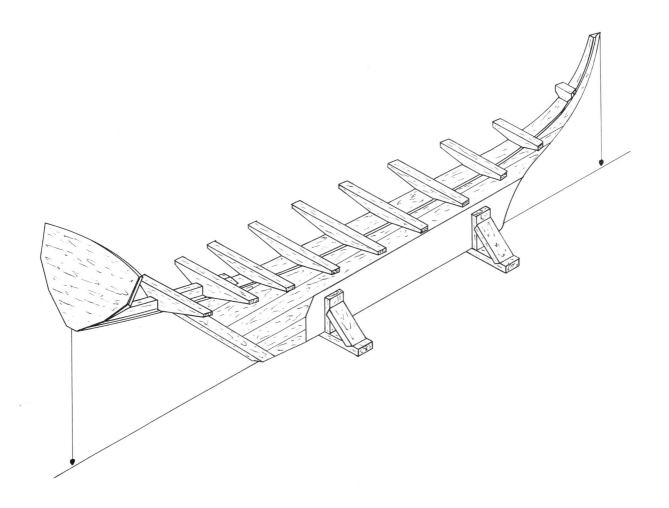

Fig 16 *Setting up the backbone, floors and transom*

as opposed to ½in. Referring to Figure 17a, it will be seen that the angles at the chine have been bisected, in other words, showing the mitre angle which will have to be cut on the ends of the three separate pieces making up each half of the frames. This line must be extended slightly beyond the width of the material to enable the mitre angle to be transferred to the edges of the frame, squared-up and drawn on the face ready for cutting.

Once cut they can be laid out on the lofting and the ply gussets made up. Referring to Figure 17b,

these can be in the form of either 1 or 2 but in any case should be uniform throughout for aesthetic reasons if nothing else. These gussets will be on the aft face of frames 0 to 5 and on the forward face of frames 6 to 10. They can be glued and screwed or nailed with Gripfast nails. Note that in each case they must overlap not less than ⅛in to allow for the bevel as in Figure 17c. The half-frame can now be turned over and supported at each end on some scrap ply to stop them tipping. The mirror half now being made on top with the sheer marks clearly shown.

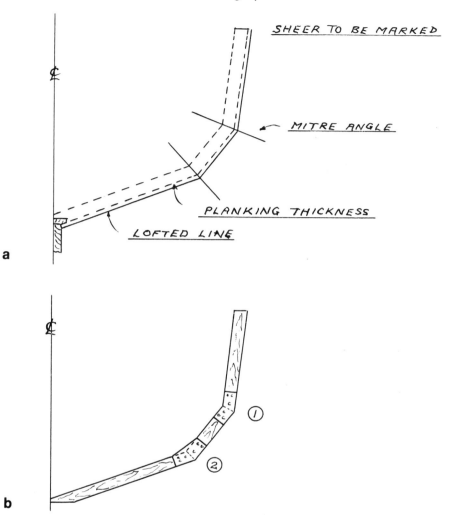

SHEER TO BE MARKED

₵

MITRE ANGLE

PLANKING THICKNESS

LOFTED LINE

a

₵

①

②

b

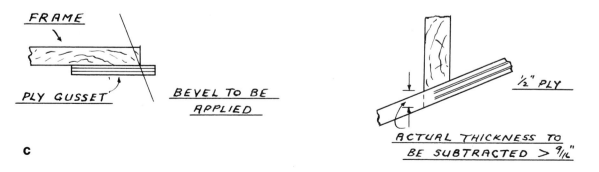

FRAME

PLY GUSSET

BEVEL TO BE APPLIED

½" PLY

ACTUAL THICKNESS TO BE SUBTRACTED > 9/16"

c

Fig 17 a, b and c

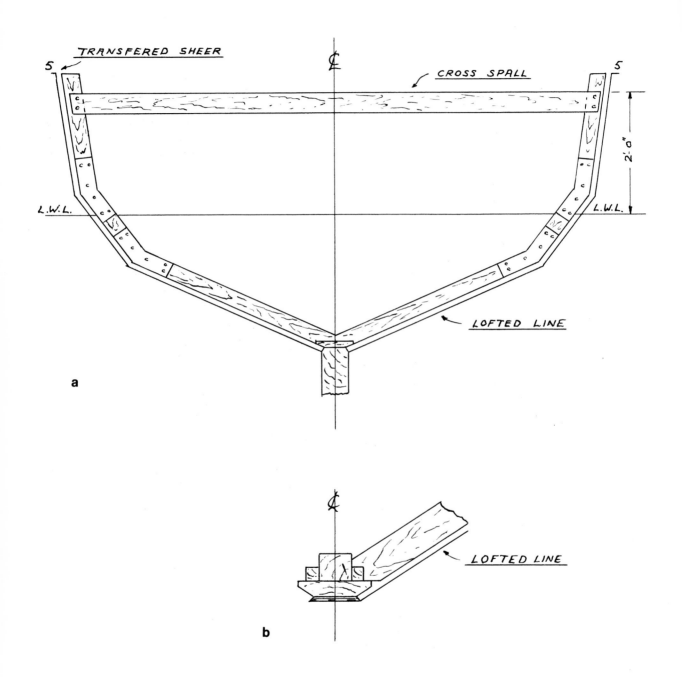

Fig 18a *(Station 5) and* **18b** *(station 9)*

To assemble the two halves ready for erection, we need a line two feet above and parallel to the waterline drawn on to the body-plan (Fig 18). This will represent the top of the cross spall. The sheer at all frames must also be transferred to their opposite side, which will enable the sheer markings to be aligned. The cross spall is best made from 4 × ¾in deal, but must on all accounts be straight, otherwise it defeats its purpose. Once it has been screwed on, a centre-line is drawn on the top edge and both faces. The centre-line should not be put on by sight but squared-up from the floor, as should the cross spall. The frame can now be carefully turned over, the bottoms lined up and a temporary cleat tacked on to what is now the forward face of the frame. This method will be adopted for all frames except 8, 9 and 10. (See Fig 2 – General Construction) These frames will butt on to each side of the horn timber as shown in Figure 18b.

When all the frames have been made up, a bevel will have to be planed on to the bottoms to enable them to sit on the hog properly. This bevel is taken off the profile lofting. Now the frames can be erected. It is good practice to first try it dry, because before final fitting there are several things that can and need to be done that are easier to do on the bench. The first thing is to put a thin saw-cut into the centre-line on the top edge of the cross spalls, about ⅛in deep. This will be used to jam the plumb-line into and also make the height adjustment quick and easy.

Once erected the frames should be plumbed both horizontally and vertically and at this stage, fastened temporally with a couple of screws, one each side. Each frame must also be braced in both directions. Horizontally by shores from the floor, and vertically by internal bracing from the cross spalls to hog or floors, whichever is most convenient (Fig 19). Before they are eventually dismantled, it is a good idea to use some form of identification on the shores and braces to help with re-erection when the time comes.

Before proceeding any further, a visual check should be made on the spalls. It is hoped that by sighting them along their top edges, they will all appear to be level and all the centre-lines line up. There always seems to be one or two that don't. If any frames are off-centre, check the bottom of the

frame and also use a spirit level on the cross spalls. The frame may need moving over a fraction. This can be done with the floor braces. If there is an error in the height, it may mean planing off the bottom of the frame or a thin packing introduced. All this can take a considerable time, but must be done step by step until all is satisfactory. If there is a major error, the only course of action is to remove the offending frame and take it back to the lofting and check there. Mistakes are easily made when setting up.

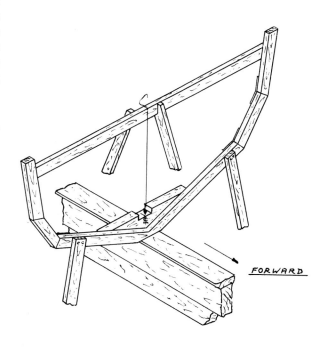

Fig 19 *Plumbing a frame and bracing to floor and hog*

FORWARD

The chines can now be checked by running a batten round; one of the lofting battens would be ideal. The batten should run round with its lower edge on the point of the chine, cramped on and then sighted round for fairness in both directions. By doing this, the centre of the chines can be drawn on to the stem and transom. At the same time, by centring the batten on each section of the frame, the amount of bevel can be measured and drawn in on the appropriate face of the frame as in Figure 20. The line of the sheer also needs checking. All the frames can now be removed, so it is back to the bench. All the bevels are now planed. It should be mentioned that the sheer marks should be transferred to the aft face to prevent them being planed off when bevelling. Pretty obvious but can be forgotten.

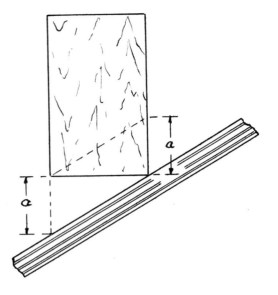

Fig 20

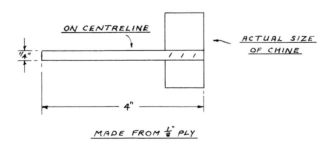

Fig 21

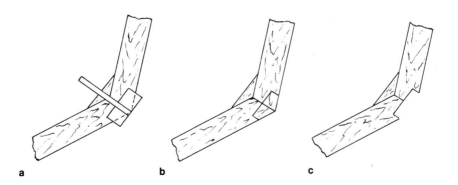

As there are some forty chine notches to cut out, a little helpful gadget will be welcome. It is made from ⅛in ply as shown in Figure 21. As can be seen, it represents the section of the chine and has a small leg glued to it with one edge through the centre-line. The leg is aligned with the mitre and the 'Tee' at the point of the chine. This is drawn around as in Figure 21a and cut out as in Figure 21c. This marking out is done on both faces, so the mitre angle is transferred on to the gussets, using a bevel. The outlines are now joined on the edge of the frames and cut out. The same applies for the gunwale, the angle of rise at the sheer being taken from the lofting.

Notches like the chines are awkward to cut out, especially where ply is used, it being very difficult to chop into with a chisel for instance. The best method is to tenon-saw the edges and then jigsaw from the gusset side. This will only leave a little timber to be chiselled away. If you are feeling brave however, it can all be done with the jigsaw and then touched up with a chisel or rasp. The transom frame must also be notched out, and after drawing in the housing, it is easier to drill a series of holes down to the ply and then chop and clean up. This method puts least strain on the transom, unless it can be shored up from a solid wall or other point.

Now all the frames can be set up finally, being screwed or bolted on. Having numbered all the bracing should make things easier. To add to the rigidity of the frames, a plank of 5 × 1in can be nailed to the cross spalls, with one edge on the centre-line. As two or three planks will be needed, they should overlap on opposite faces by two frames to form a continuous straight line. Everything should now be ready for the chines, except the stem which is best dealt with later.

Making Up and Fitting the Chines

The chine timber will be scarfed, and as those in the example are 2 × 1in (finished size) the scarfs will be 8in long. These can be cut with the jigsaw and finished on the bench (Fig 22). By using a block, as shown, a good square feather edge can be achieved. Before gluing, this faying surface must be roughened or scored with a chisel to provide a key for the adhesive. When gluing and before cramping, it is advisable to staple the feather edges down, wrap in polythene and use short blocks of wood to make sure that the edges are firmly down (Fig 23). Also sight the scarfs to detect any kinks since they cannot be rectified later. Before fitting the chines, the appropriate bevels can be applied. Station lines are drawn on the sides and a centre-line struck on the face. Dimension 'a' as in Figure 24a drawn in and all points joined up. The bevels are planed on, but always as before, give yourself some leeway. By fitting the chine as in Figure 24b, you can achieve the same results.

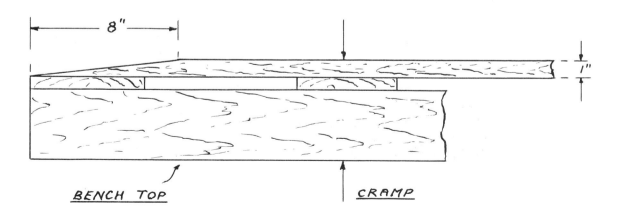

BENCH TOP   CRAMP

8"

1"

Fig 22

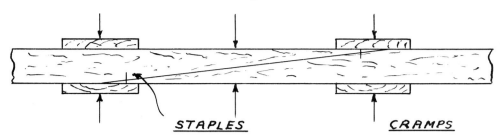

STAPLES   CRAMPS

Fig 23

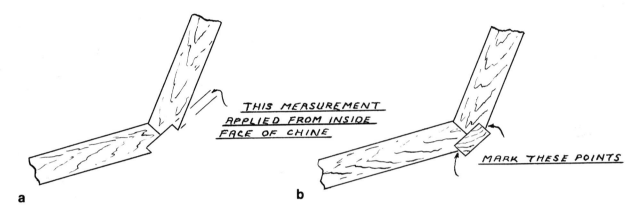

THIS MEASUREMENT
APPLIED FROM INSIDE
FACE OF CHINE

MARK THESE POINTS

a   b

Fig 24

A dry run can now be made, when the stem housing can be cut, every joint checked and the chines and gunwales cut to length to fit into the transom and stem (Fig 25). The chines and gunwales are now drilled and countersunk for screws. When fitting finally, alternate sides should be fitted in order to reduce the strain on the frames. Another point to remember as you fasten, is to check that the frames have not been displaced slightly out of square from the centre-line due to the pressure exerted on them by the chines or gunwales. This may be more evident at the ends. Any offending frames should be gently tapped into position. If the upper chine is fitted first and any anomaly dealt with, there should be no more problems.

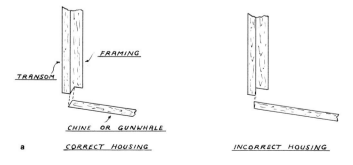

FRAMING

TRANSOM

CHINE OR GUNWHALE

a   CORRECT HOUSING

INCORRECT HOUSING

Fig 25a Housing at transom

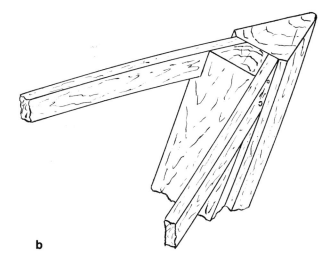

b

Fig 25b *Housing at stem*

but any fault in the bevel at this point can distort the batten, so care is needed. This job can be tedious but should nevertheless be approached in a methodical manner. If at chine and frame the chine happens to be slightly proud, it should be planed off in the direction of the frame, rather than in the direction of the chine, as shown in Figure 26. The chines, gunwales and hog come next, although the gunwale should need little or no fairing, only perhaps forward where a little change in the flair occurs. Considerable care is needed fairing-in the chines, and again this must be done methodically using the straight-edge. The 'apex' of the chine must run fair, so keep an eye on this as you proceed. The effect is shown in Figure 27. It cannot be corrected with the planking. When the overlap at 'a' is planed and faired off, the chine reverts back to its original unfair line. The hull is now ready for planking.

Fig 26 *Fairing the chine at the frame*

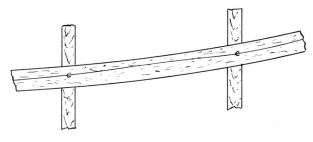

UNFAIR CHINE

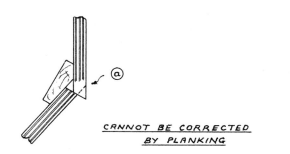

CANNOT BE CORRECTED
BY PLANKING

Fig 27

Fairing the Hull

Use an 8ft length of ½in ply about 3in wide, together with a 4ft straight-edge and concentrate on the frames, stem, rabbet, hog and transom first. When testing the frame bevels, the batten should cover about four frames, so an extra hand may be required. Cramping one end is possible,

Chapter 7

Planking – Chine Hull

Before discussing the planking, possibly the next step in the building process, it is worth considering the idea of building in all the accommodation first. I did this with my own boat and it was completely successful. There are considerable advantages to be had, among them being the ease of fitting bulkheads, engine, sterntube and lockers etc., with complete freedom of access. Also you are able to paint the many places that become inaccessible when the hull is planked. No crawling up those quarter-berths and getting covered in paint.

To take this a step further, when planking is made up, the inside surface can be painted before the final fitting, thus giving 'instant' finish. Worth thinking about!

Planking

Planking should start at the hog and stem, working aft and alternating each side. A template must be made up using the near maximum length of the ply and measured along the lower chine, see Figure 28 for a guide to the planking layout. This can be drawn on to the lofting. The two main criteria are maximum use of the ply and avoiding the butts coming too close to each other. Having measured along the lower chine, a batten is stapled on at right-angles to the hog, from which a template is made up. The top edge is taken to the centre of the chine. This template, which will be quite large, should be well braced to avoid distortion once removed.

An example is shown in Figure 29. This can now be taken to the cutting bench and the panel cut out. The lower edge can be cut to the line, but the top edge should have about ¼in left on to allow some leeway in fitting the lower edge into the rebate. When offering the panel into place, it will need shoring up from the floor, together with cramps on the chine and stem. The lower edge can now be checked for fitting and any high spots marked in and faired off. This may well need to be done several times before a good fit is obtained.

It must be stressed here that when fitting the panels at this stage, they must 'seat' everywhere properly, otherwise you will encounter considerable problems later. Having obtained a good fit, the panel can now have hog, stem, frame and chine outlined on the back to be used as a guide to drilling for fastenings. Holes for the fastenings can now be drilled from the reverse side and then countersunk on the face side for the screws or Gripfast nails. Screw centres should be in the order of 4in centres.

This panel can now be screwed on dry, with only enough screws to hold it in position and bedded properly. The first butt strap can now be fitted dry. The minimum width not less than 4in and the same thickness as the planking. It must be made to fit snugly between hog and chine. Due to the angle made by the edge of the chine, it may well have to be slid in sideways, or alternatively secured in place before fitting the planks. This method will be easier and also ensure a better fit, but will entail an accurate marking out.

We can now make up and fit its opposite number. Well, at least we have a template made up, but here comes the crunch – it almost certainly will not fit! Try it by all means. You may get away with tacking short pieces of ply on here and there or by making little notes – 'plus a bit' or 'minus a bit' – but by the time you get this modified template on to the ply, things can get a little confusing. Generally speaking it is better to pull your template apart and make a new one.

All the remaining panels can now be made up to the transom, fitting the butt straps as you proceed. As mentioned before, a slight excess being left at the chine for fairing through and providing the correct mitre angle for the next section of planking to fit to. The fairing of this narrow edge is best done with a rebate plane and the correct angle of the mitre being gauged from the frame mitres. Watch out for knuckles and stray fingers when passing the frames!

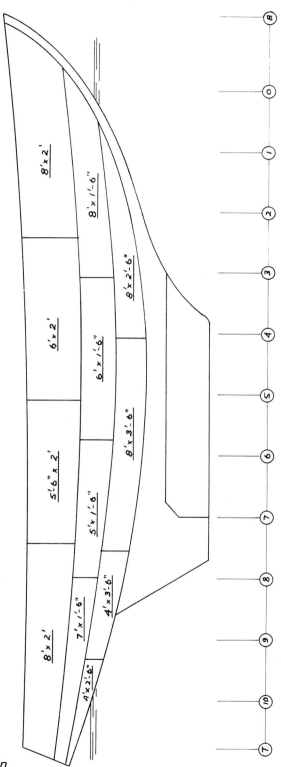

Fig 28 Layout of the ply skin

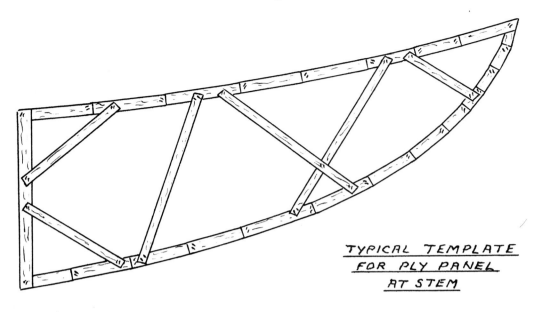

TYPICAL TEMPLATE
FOR PLY PANEL
AT STEM

TYPICAL BUTTSTRAP

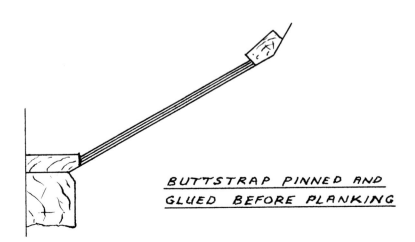

BUTTSTRAP PINNED AND
GLUED BEFORE PLANKING

Fig 29

All the planking can now be removed ready for the final fitting. As mentioned at the beginning of the chapter, it is good practice to paint the inside surface to a finish, as it is extremely difficult once the accommodation is fitted. The guide lines for the fastenings show the limits of the paint line. These lines can safely be overpainted – just.

When considering the bottom planking, determine which panels should be painted with bilge paint or perhaps white in the heads compartment for example. Whatever you decide, the planking can now be glued and screwed or Gripfast nailed. Using nails at the chines can prove difficult due to the 'bounce' when hammering and is therefore difficult to set the nails properly. They are quite ideal where the backing is solid. If the accommodation has not been fitted, it is possible to use nails on the chines with a helper inside holding a dolly.

The rest of the planking can now follow in the same manner, completing the middle chine before going on to the topsides. The edge at the sheer should be faired off ready to receive the deck panels.

The only other job remaining is to stop up all the screw and nail heads. Where nails have been used, they will need to be punched down below the surface to give the stopping a chance to stay put. Needless to say, all the joints must also be stopped. There are several marine stoppings but my favourite is Davids Isopon P38™ car body filler. It is easy to apply, dries quickly and has minimal shrinkage. After filling the screw holes it is best to scrape off the surplus with a sharp scraper. This will show up the low spots as a slightly darker colour and quickly identify the holes where further filling is required.

This now completes the hull except for the waterline and boot top.

Waterline and Boot Top

Ascertain the height of the waterline from the lofting. A horizontal batten is then set up at each end, similar to a sawing horse. This must be set up with a spirit level and extend a few inches beyond the maximum beam at waterline. Set up a string-line parallel to the centre-line and just touching the hull. Make fast the aft end. Here you will need a helper armed with small panel pins and a light hammer.

As you draw the string-line round towards your stem, your helper should tap in pins just below the line to stop it sliding down the hull. The line can be pulled out and then back in to make sure the pins are correctly placed and doing their job. Once the forward section has been done, the procedure is applied to the aft section. The transom area is generally the most difficult because the waterline here changes dramatically in direction. After completing both sides, sighting by eye from both ends will reveal any errors, which can be corrected by eye also. This line can now be pencilled in using a batten and afterwards by scoring with a fine tenon-saw.

Use the same procedures for a boot top. If it is to be parallel to the waterline, you merely raise the two horizontal battens. Aesthetically, a boot top looks far more pleasing if it is raised slightly towards the stem and transom. This can be achieved by using angled pieces of ply cramped on to the guides and by trial and error a suitable angle can be determined to produce an unobtrusive curve to both ends. This line should also be cut in.

Photo 1

Photo 2

Photos 1 and 2 Here the interior accommodation has already been fitted and painted and now the planking is underway. Note that the keel has not been finally added to this example – a look at the height of the roof should give you the reason.

Photo 3 *Here, to keep your spirits up, is a view you can look forward to when all is complete.*

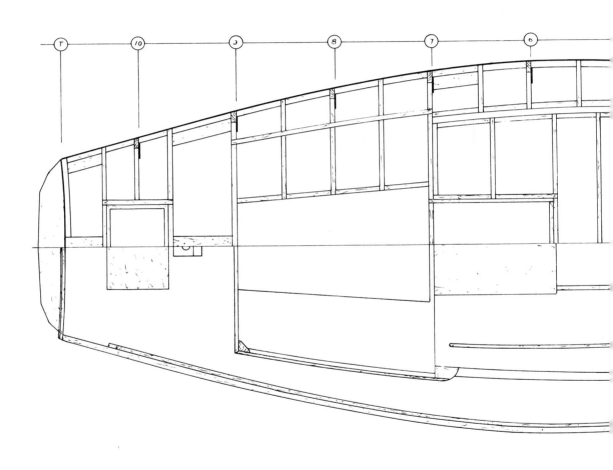

Fig 30 *Deck plan of Goosander 27*

Deck Structure

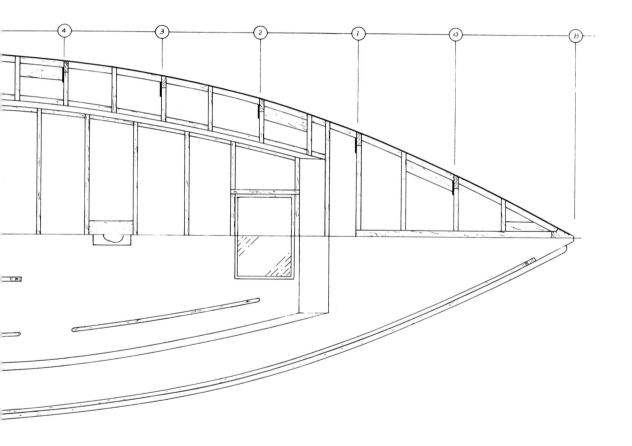

Chapter 8
Deck Structure

Deck Beams

We can now concentrate on the deck structure, comprising deck beams, cockpit, carlins, hatches and cabin coamings, together with hand-rails, toe-rails and rubbing strakes. An overview can be gleaned from Figure 2 and also the deck-plan illustrated by Figure 30. Here you will also find an indication of the crown of the deck beams, in this case ½in per foot length of the longest beam which is 8ft 3in. We shall call it 8ft for practical purposes. The longest beam should be drawn out on a piece of ply. The laminating board should be of sufficient length to allow it to be drawn on it, so that angle irons can be screwed directly in place.

The method used is shown in Figure 31. If sawn beams are to be used, then a template will be required using 9mm ply and also representing the depth of the beam.

Since the deck beams will be required first, their lamination will be ongoing. If the angle irons on the jigs are 6in high, then two beams can be made up in one operation as shown in Figure 32. (The drawing illustrates cramps by arrows.)

Laminated beams must have a minimum of at least four laminations or they will tend to spring too much when they are released from the jig. In the example, with 2in deep beams, four ½in laminations will suffice.

A pleasing interior effect can be achieved with the use of two contrasting timbers, for example mahogany and pine glued alternately. Looks good and creates no additional work.

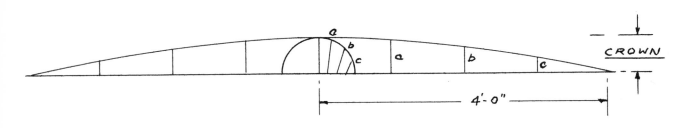

Fig 31 *Layout of deck beam*

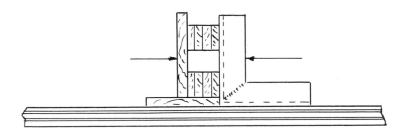

Fig 32 *Laminating two deck beams at once*

When six beams have been made up, the housing in the gunwales can be cut-in ready to accept the fitting. These housings should be cut for each individual beam – essential if they have been hand-made, as they will surely vary slightly in width. None of us are perfect! However, if they can be passed through a 'thicknesser', you will be on safer ground. The method illustrated in Fig 33 is the simplest but remember that the use of a sliding square with combined 'bubble' is essential. There are of course alternatives such as dovetailing, but try and keep it simple.

The joint shown in Figure 33, although simple to cut out, seems to cause problems in marking out, so a brief description will not go amiss. Once the beam has been laid across the gunwales, the width of the beam should be marked on top of the gunwale. This width should be transferred down vertically and a horizontal line drawn at the depth of the beam and then measured from the highest side. It will therefore be forward between station 0 to 5 and aft from stations 6 to 10. Two saw cuts can now be made and the joint chiselled out, making the platform about ¼in deep. The beam is now replaced over the top of the two housings and points a, b, c and d transferred up vertically using the combined square and level. The beam must be manoeuvred in both directions to allow the square to locate points b and c. Join all four points and cut the lines. The beam should now drop in perfectly.

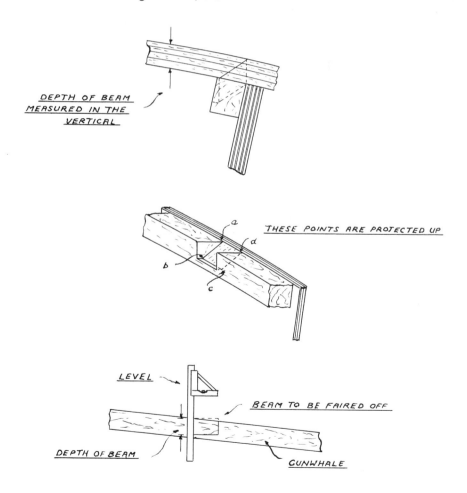

DEPTH OF BEAM MEASURED IN THE VERTICAL

THESE POINTS ARE PROJECTED UP

a
d
b
c

LEVEL

BEAM TO BE FAIRED OFF

DEPTH OF BEAM

GUNWHALE

Fig 33

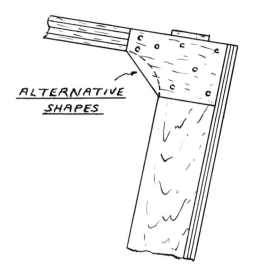

SHEER MARK

ALTERNATIVE SHAPES

Fig 34

You may now observe that the configuration of the beam creates a potential wedge that when slightly over length and forced, would push the gunwales apart – therefore better to be slightly under width than over. The beams that locate at the frames are best marked as shown in Figure 34. Cut the beam to about ½in short of the gunwale, line up the ends of the beams with the top of the gunwale and cramp into position. Scribe the inner face of the frame onto the beam and square a line across the top of the beam, cut to length.

Now glue and screw a web (Fig 34), not forgetting the bevel required where it meets the planking. The dotted line shows an alternative profile. Having cut the beams to length but before fitting, the underside should be radiused, but stopped some 4in from either end. If a router of ½in is at hand, use it to create a superior, even finish. The cross spalls should not be removed until the

appropriate beam is fitted to eliminate any slight chance of the hull moving.

Deck Hatches

Where a deck hatch is to be sited, the half beam should be omitted until the hatch carlin is fitted. The joints that are used are simple half-lap or stopped as in Figure 35. The carlin is let-in vertically so that its inboard edge is flush with the fore end of the beam. These edges will be removed later when fairing-in. When chopping out for stopped housings, it is essential to shore the beam and to only take out two laminations. When sawn beams are used, half the depth of the beam is removed. The king plank, like the carlins, can be half lapped into the beams. When all the beams are in place, the cabin and cockpit carlins can be approached. The cockpit carlins are straight and can be dealt with in the same manner as the deck hatches.

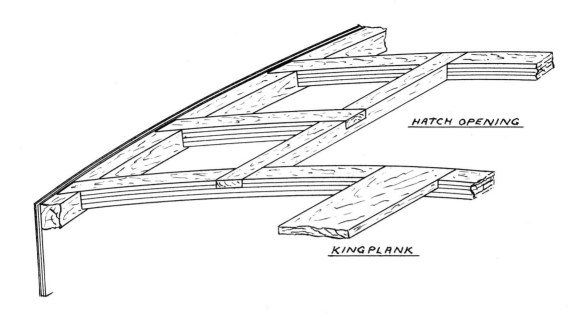

HATCH OPENING

KINGPLANK

JOINTS AT CARLIN AND BEAM

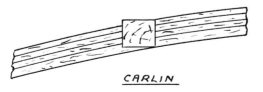

CARLIN

Fig 35

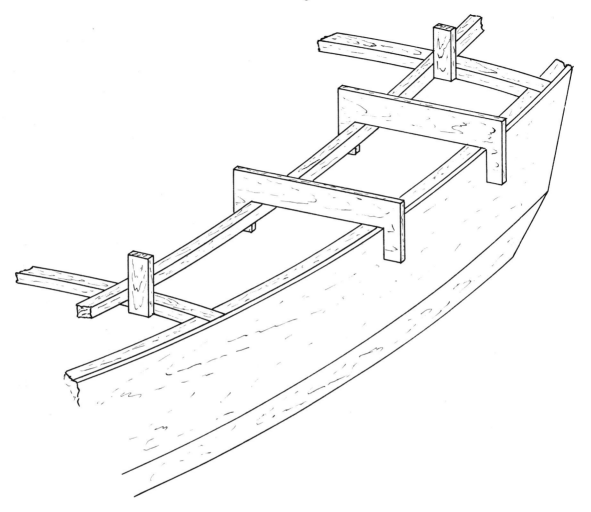

Fig 36 *Marking out position of carlin for length and housing*

Cabin Carlins

The cabin carlins will require more attention because they are curved in both profile and plan and depending on the method you choose, may be canted to provide tumblehome for the cabin sides. As can be seen in Figure 36, two stops are cramped on the main beams at the appropriate deck width, with two or even three ply cramps to maintain its curvature. Sash cramps can be used to pull the carlin down. Mark the housings at each end together with the length. If the carlins are to be canted, mark the joint as shown in Figure 37 and merely draw them in at the required angle using a bevel. Having marked out both ends, staple a couple of thin battens on the marks and sight them to check that the angle at both ends is the same. After refitting and pulling into shape, a long beam can be laid across between the gunwales and all the housings marked out and then cut on the bench. Now fit the side-deck beams. Keep the two stops in place or it will prove difficult to locate the ends into their housings and at the same time bend the carlin into shape.

Before starting the cabin sides, the entire deck structure should be faired, including any frames which may be slightly proud. If this is not done, then difficulty will be met in the vicinity of the cabin sides and particularly the side-decks.

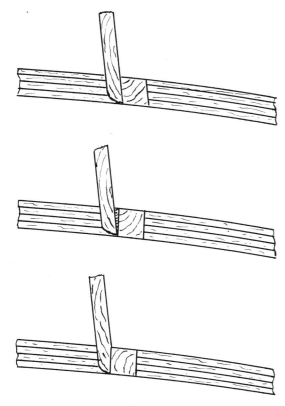

Fig 37 *Various options for fitting carlin*

Cabin Sides

A template should be made using the height and shape as per the construction details. Incorporate the window outlines into the template. Insert the verticals with the use of a level. Figure 38 illustrates the type of template to make and it will also be noted that a wedge will be glued to the forward beam to produce the required angle of tumblehome to the fore end of the cabin. If the top edge of the template is somewhat undulating, it can be smoothed when marking out. Mark the radiused corners of the windows with compasses. The whole unit can now be cut, including the window holes, and allowing extra for the bevels.

Fitting can be tricky single-handed so grab a helper. Locate the aft end first and cramp it lightly and induce a curve so that it can be pushed into place. This may need doing several times if the bevel is not quite right or has been cut over-length.

Now approach the other side where yet again you may find that your first template may not fit. If you must make another template, forget the window outlines because there are only likely to be two differences, the length or the curve of the carlin. You can use the original to draw in the windows later.

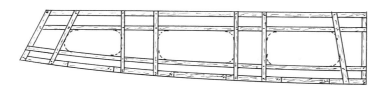

TEMPLATE OF CABIN COAMING
SHOWING WINDOWS

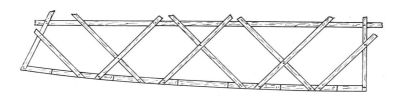

TEMPLATE TO BE COMPLETED
ON COAMING MATERIAL

Fig 38

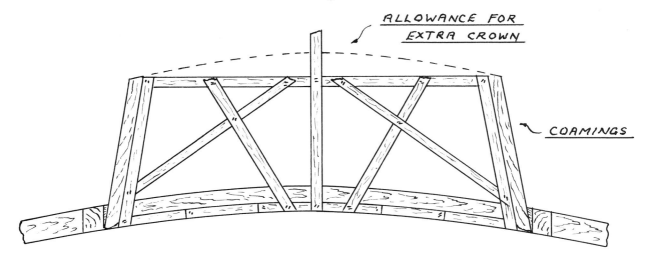

TYPICAL FORE END TEMPLATE

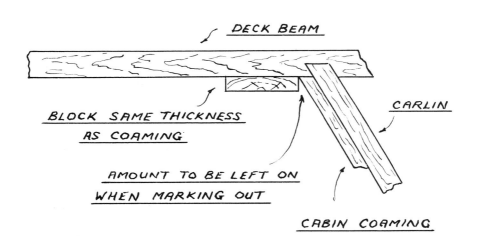

Fig 39

Before the final fitting, the window openings can be radiused and rebated to accept the perspex window material and all the window fastenings drilled and countersunk. After a final sanding they can be glued and screwed into place. Another job at this stage is to create the bevel required at the top edge. The construction drawing will reveal if the crown of the cabin beams is different to that of the deck beams, a template will be necessary if that is the case.

The fore end of the cabin is treated in the same manner as the sides. Remember to allow sufficient material for the crown, which because of the tumblehome will be more than that of the coachroof beams. If we take our example, an additional ¾in would be left on. This surplus will be dealt with later. A template as shown in Figure 39 is quite adequate with the radius being drawn in on the material. The side bevels must be allowed for. As with all bevels they should be taken off the work and transferred onto a piece of ply, or more simply found as in Figure 39. This is pretty basic stuff and perhaps obvious, but it may act as a timely reminder.

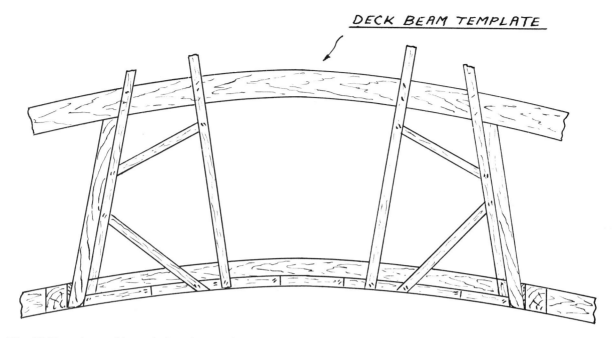

DECK BEAM TEMPLATE

Fig 40 *Template with main hatch opening*

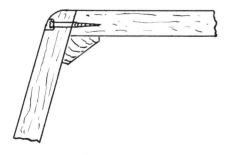

Fig 41 *Alternative coaming arrangements*

The fore end can now be fastened and glued, both onto the beam and through the cabin sides. Again, radius and pre-drill before final fitting. The aft end is next. The template shown in Figure 40 is best made in one piece, using the beam template to obtain the correct camber. The main-hatch opening must be measured accurately making due allowance for the washboard slides and with battens stapled on to represent the opening. The two sections can now be traced off on to the material and cut to shape and fitted.

There are other methods of finishing at the corners and shown in Figure 41. Here you cut short and introduce corner posts that give a solid professional appearance. This can be supplemented by a further cover post inside as illustrated.

The carlins are fitted next and when so doing, must be fitted a little proud at the top to allow for chamfering off. As with the coamings a beam or template is used. Having marked out the beam spacings, the housings are cut in as for deck beams and all the beams fitted. A beam should also be fastened to the fore end, and as there is considerable bevel it is advisable to use five laminations in order to keep the proportion. The whole can now be faired off leaving the forward end till last. A batten can now be laid onto the beams and up to the fore end and a series of tick marks made. This will give the shape required. A nice effect is produced if the carlins are radiused in between the beams, stopping 3in or 4in short of the beams.

Deck Pads

Before we touch on the deck planking there is one important job to be done and that is fitting the deck pads. There will be a number of these pads to put in and this is the easiest time. The following all require pads – stanchions, pulpit, pushpit, chain pipe, deck-eyes, sheet tracks, deck fillers, rudder tube, winches (mounted on the coachroof) mast pad, mainsheet horse and perhaps other deck fittings. The pads need to be substantial and well-fastened. Once a list is made, the positions of each pad should be drawn on a deck plan which should be fully dimensioned showing the location and size of each pad. Also at this stage, draw in the location of all the deck and side-deck beams and also hull frames and beams. This is most important to locate fastenings and for handrails etc, once things disappear below the deck ply.

Decking

Decking with ply is quite straightforward, but will need planning to prevent wastage of material. The usual templates will be necessary but unlike the hull, the panels will be butted and joined on the beams. Butt-straps would be unsightly under the deckhead. A typical layout is shown in Figure 42 and 42a shows the method of butting the panels at the fore end of the cabin. This also applies at the aft end of the cockpit coaming. It is desirable to have the grain running in a fore and aft direction, as the ply is slightly more flexible across the grain.

The coachroof poses a slightly more difficult problem because, due to its width, the ply must be laid with the grain running athwartships. 12mm ply does not bend readily in this direction. In order to solve the problem it is better to use two sheets of 6mm ply. These panels like those on the deck, are butted on to a beam and must be

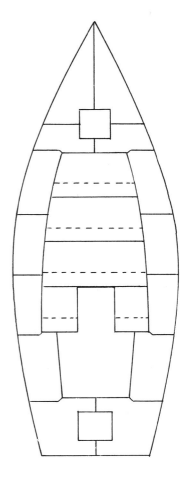

Fig 42 Typical ply deck layout showing coachroof double skinned

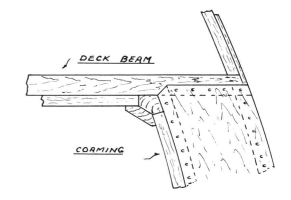

Fig 42a Ply deck at corners

glued and fastened there. The second layer of joints overlapped by one beam length. The outboard edges are nailed or screwed to the coamings. Before stapling the second layer on the coachroof, have a box of cardboard squares ready to use under the staple heads, this not only protects the ply, but also makes the removal of the staples much easier. It is a great advantage to paint the deckhead before fixing.

Figures 43, 43a, b and c show some details of the deck hatches, main hatch, hatch openings and grab-rail, more clearly than I can explain them. The corners of the hatches would look better if dovetailed, but the method I have shown is simple and practical. Positioning the main hatch can be a bit of a puzzle and can only be done by offering into place – and then by lifting on either side, the brass runners can be slid into place. At this stage the runners only need to be drilled at each end. Once the hatch is centred, the runners can be temporarily screwed and the hatch moved backwards and forwards to make sure it runs smoothly. If all is well, close the hatch fully and mark the centre for a screw about ¼in forward of the hatch, then push the hatch forward and do likewise aft of the hatch. The whole can now be removed and the slides fully drilled and countersunk. When refitted the hatch should run smoothly.

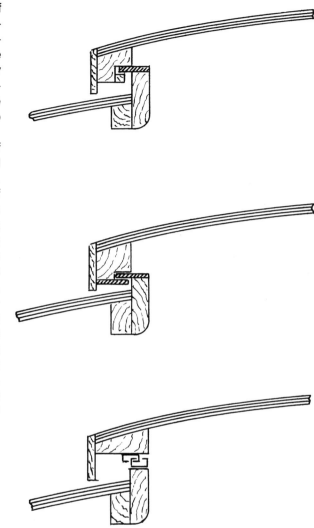

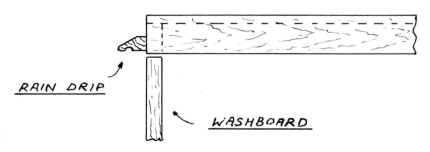

RAIN DRIP

WASHBOARD

Fig 43 *Main hatch arrangements*

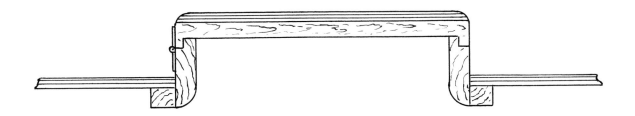

SIMPLE FORM OF HATCH

WATERTIGHT HATCH

DRAINHOLES IN OUTER FRAME

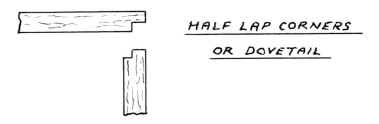

HALF LAP CORNERS

OR DOVETAIL

Fig 43a Deck hatches

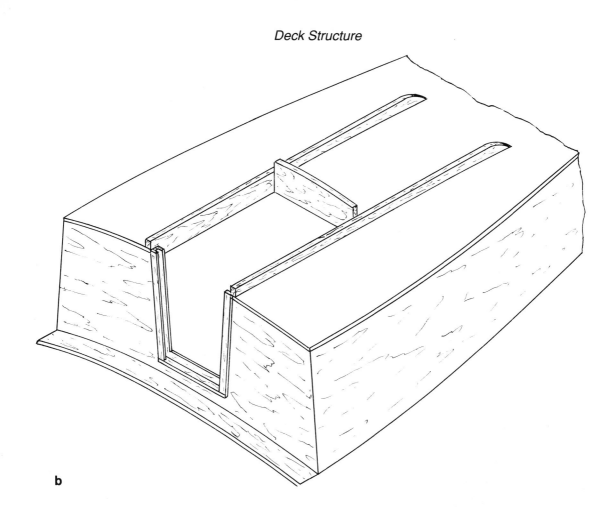

b

TYPICAL ARRANGEMENT
FOR MAIN HATCH

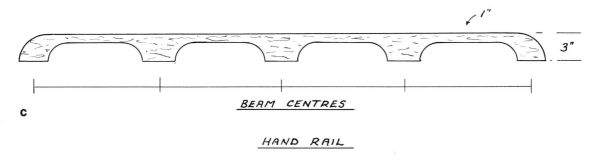

1"

3"

BEAM CENTRES

c

HAND RAIL

Figs 43b and c

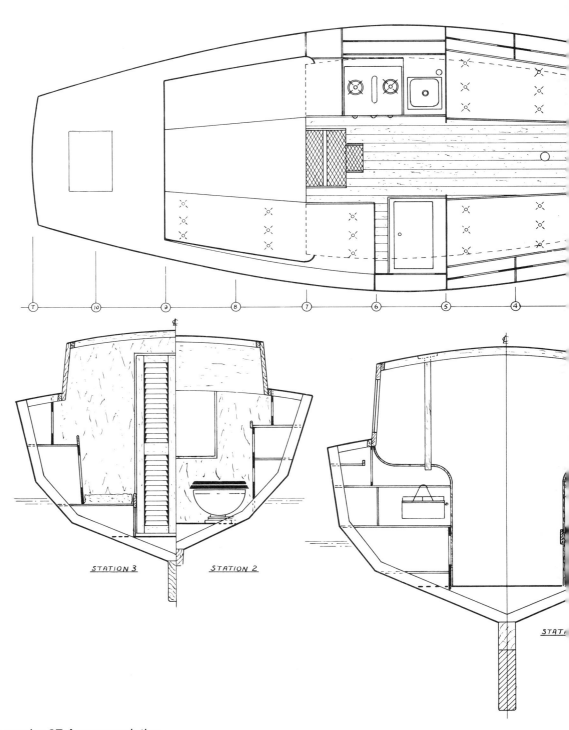

Fig 44 *Goosander 27 Accommodation*

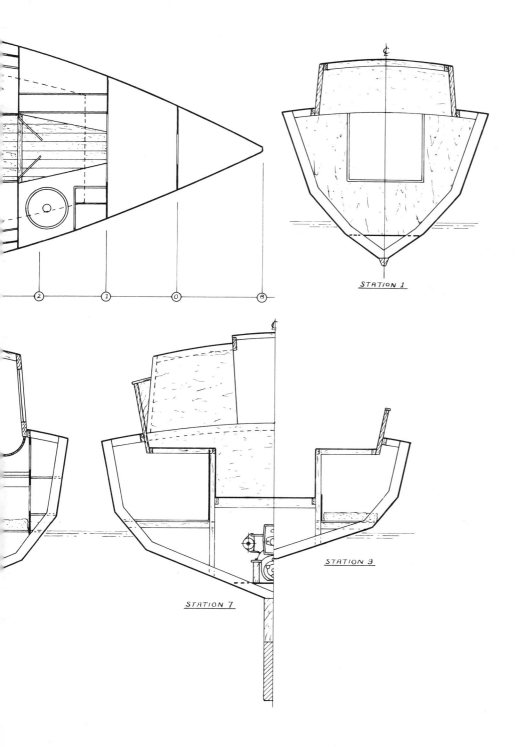

STATION 1

STATION 9

STATION 7

Profile view

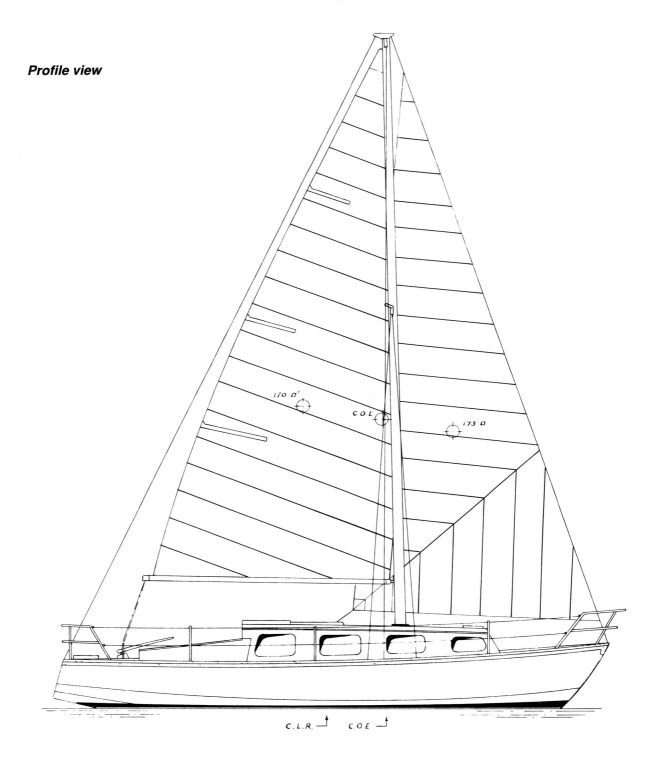

Fig 45 Sail plan of Goosander 27

Fig 45 ahead view

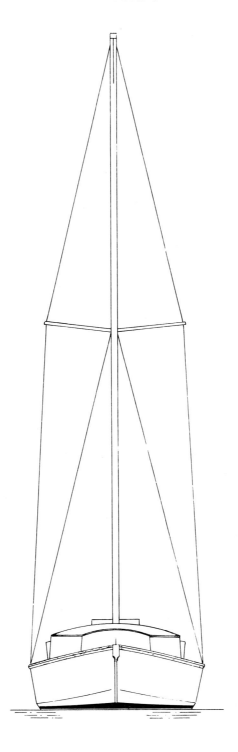

Chapter 9

Accommodation

Accommodation is a combination of good basic joinery and finish. It can make or mar a boat. Attention to detail is paramount, with much considered thought given to access for skin-fittings, pipework, wiring, keel bolts, sterngear, rudder gear and fuel/water tanks. All too often these are buried away and forgotten until the day comes when something goes wrong. Seacocks must be totally accessible, with sufficient room about them for spanners and screwdriver when they have to be removed for servicing or to repair in an emergency at sea. All this is of course basic common-sense, but for some reason seems to be neglected in many boats.

Accommodation should not only be functional for the inhabitants of the vessel, but it should also provide a great deal of stiffness to the hull and additional support to the deck.

This chapter is applicable whether or not the hull has been planked. However, if the hull has not been planked it may be necessary to use some ½in ply to represent the hull shape in such instances as shelves or where members need to meet the hull. Unless the item is structural it is often advisable to leave a small gap between fitting and hull to allow a circulation of air and to let condensation run down into the bilge.

Bulkheads and Sole

All the bulkheads can now be fitted first and should preferably be double skinned with cleating between. This not only strengthens them but also makes for a substantial appearance. The ply can either be glued or screwed to the cleating or glued and pinned. Pinning is neater since the pins can be punched in and the holes stopped.

Once all the bulkheads have been fitted, the sole can be laid down, with cleating being fixed to the bulkheads where needed to support the sole. The sole should be carried out to, but not touching the hull. Trap doors must be cut to allow access to keel bolts and skin fittings. The sole should be well protected at this stage. so staple down some thick cardboard.

All the cleating for the basic accommodation structure can be fixed to the sole and work on the interior started in earnest. Have plenty of cleating to hand. If you anticipate needing 100ft, order 200ft. Interiors gobble up cleating at an alarming rate. ¾ × ¾in softwood is quite adequate, providing that it is treated with preservative or well painted.

All minor bulkheads, horizontal or vertical surfaces must be positioned using a level. This is far safer than measuring up or down from something else, which may not be level or vertical. It does happen sometimes, usually to shelves or bunk tops which will not sit properly or tip at one corner. With this prospect in mind, all floors should be checked for level in both directions. If one is slightly low, a veneer can be glued on. There is nothing worse or more annoying than walking on a cabin sole that gives or squeaks.

Timber

The timber that is chosen for the trim should contrast with the main material. If teak or sapele-faced ply is being used for construction, then a lighter colour for the trim will complement it well. In my boat, as will be seen from the photographs, I used sapele faced ply and wych elm for the trim. Some ideas are illustrated in Figures 46 and 47. I found a quantity of slightly damaged sapele-faced door skins. These were 6ft 6in × 2ft 6in × 3mm and out of twenty of these, only two had slight water stains. After I had finished a certain part of the interior it was veneered with sapele. This was glued and stapled on using cardboard squares to protect the surface. The pinholes made by the staples soon disappear under a few coats of varnish. By using this method, I was able to use 9mm exterior grade ply as the carcass material and as the veneer is quite thin and easy to plane, a pleasingly tight joint can be made.

Photo 4 *Flooring as shown in Figure 46. Note access to engine seacock below gash box, the floor lifts for servicing.*

Boatbuilding in Wood

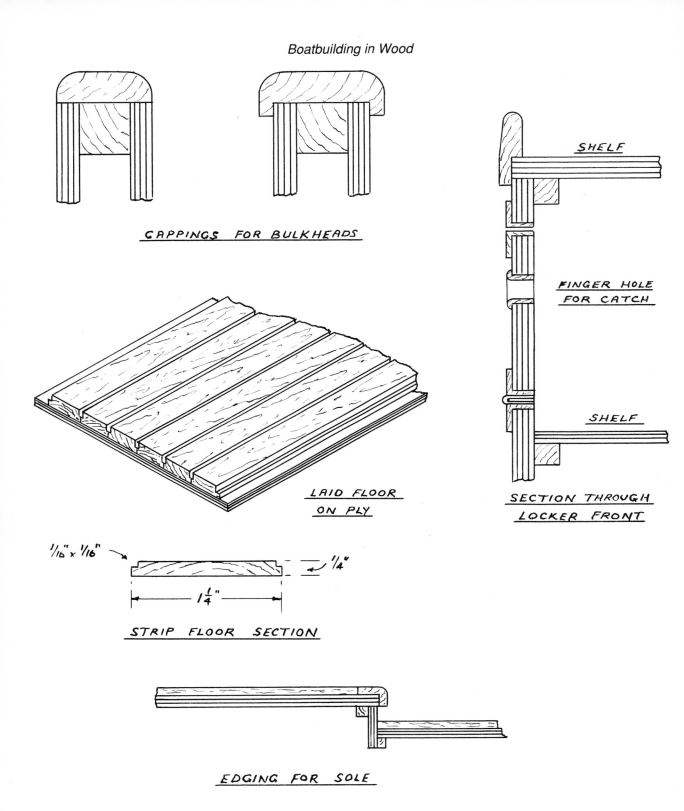

CAPPINGS FOR BULKHEADS

SHELF

FINGER HOLE
FOR CATCH

SHELF

SECTION THROUGH
LOCKER FRONT

LAID FLOOR
ON PLY

$1/16'' \times 1/16''$

$1/4''$

$1\frac{1}{4}''$

STRIP FLOOR SECTION

EDGING FOR SOLE

Fig 46 *Some useful sections*

80

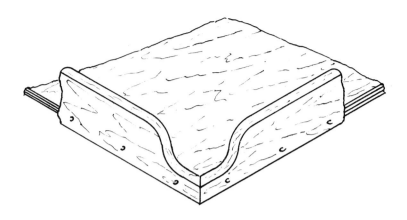

FINISHING FIDDLES ON A CORNER

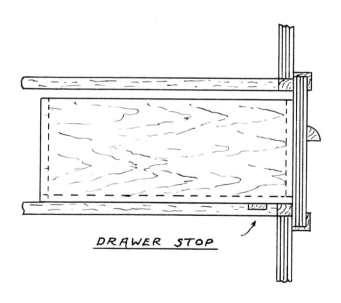

DRAWER STOP

SECTION THROUGH DRAWER

Fig 47

A question often asked and not readily answered is 'Which way should the grain run?' Basically it should run in the direction of the panel's longest axis. However, even if bulkheads are wider than they are high, the grain here should be vertical. For bunk fronts and backs the grain would run horizontally. However, a study of the sliding doors behind the cooker shown in Photo 5 confounds this theory. My reasoning here was based on a well-known saying in boat building – 'What looks right, usually is right'. I rest my case.

When cutting out locker doors, every effort should be made to retain the flow of the grain once the door is fitted. This can be achieved by cutting the blank down by the same amount off each side, and not to cut all off from either the top or one side only. Figure 48 shows how this is done in practice and can be seen to good effect in Photo 6. When parts of the interior are completed, it is good practice to sand down, stop up pin holes etc and then apply a coat of clear sealer. This will keep the grain free of dust and general contamination from finger marks and other stains that can be difficult to sand out.

During the construction of the interior you should plan the cable and pipe runs. Holes and runs are much easier to put in at this stage rather than later. There are few things more irritating than trying to drill a hole in the corner of a finished locker, especially if it is for a two inch pipe. Water pipes, bilge pipe, transducer cable, gas pipe for the cooker, battery leads and fuel pipe all need careful attention. Routing and planning at an early stage is essential.

Photo 5 *Galley and Engine Box*

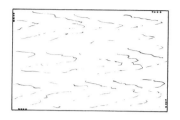

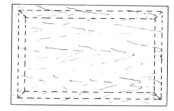

DOOR MARKED OUT AND
DRILLED FOR JIGSAW

CUT OUT AND LINED

DOOR BLANK MARKED OUT
WITH ALLOWANCE FOR EDGING
AND WORKING GAP

Fig 48

Photo 6 *Showing the grain on the backrest running through*

Photo 7 *A pleasant light and airy cabin*

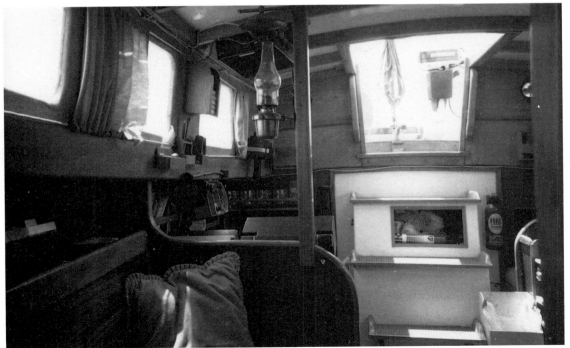

Photo 8 *General view looking aft*

Photo 9 *Chart table and instruments*

Photo 10 *Showing various types of trim*

Photo 11 *A few useful boxes*

Round Bilge Construction – Setting Up

Unlike the chine hull, this variety must be built upside-down. All the moulds are set up on a substantial frame, secured to the floor. However, first things first, and so back to the lofting as described in Chapter Three.

Body-plan

The body-plan must have the planking thickness taken-off and drawn in, preferably with a coloured felt-tip pen, together with a section of the hog, taken from the profile and half-breadth plan (Fig 8). Once all the relevant information has been drawn on the body-plan it can be traced off.

The best material to use is tracing film which is stable and strong. You will have to join at least two pieces together to cover the whole of the body-plan. Wide transparent tape of the type used to repair cracked glass is ideal, or clear sticky tape can also be used. As with the chine-hull frames, a suitable line should be used to represent the top of

the cross spalls. In the example, 4WL would be suitable. The entire body-plan can now be transferred to the mould material.

Moulds

The moulds are cut from ¾in ply, preferably birch, but Douglas Fir of a reasonable quality will suffice. Two sheets are nailed together, thus allowing two mirror halves to be cut. The tracing is now transferred to the ply, pricking through one mould at a time and allowing 4in for their width. This will require a certain amount of juggling to obtain the most economic use of the material. When one mould is pricked through it can be lined-in with a batten, together with its width, number and datum marks and should appear as in Figure 50. If great care is used when jigsawing out, there should be no need to fair these edges. You will also be pleased to know that these moulds do not require a bevel.

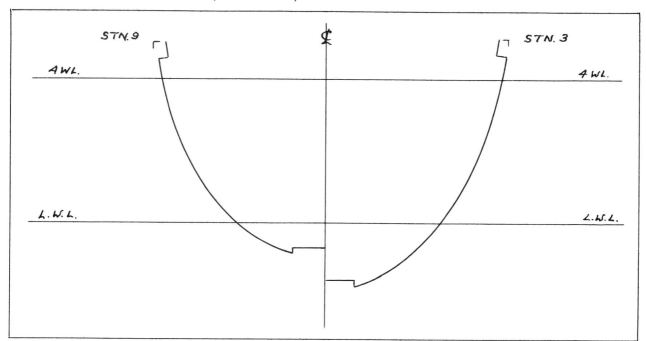

Fig 49 *Tracing-off moulds 3 and 9. Notched for gunwale and hog*

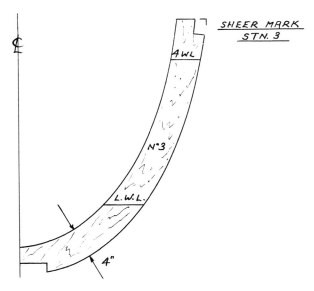

SHEER MARK
STN. 3

AWL

C̶L

N°3

L.W.L.

4"

AS DRAWN ON MOULD MATERIAL

Fig 50

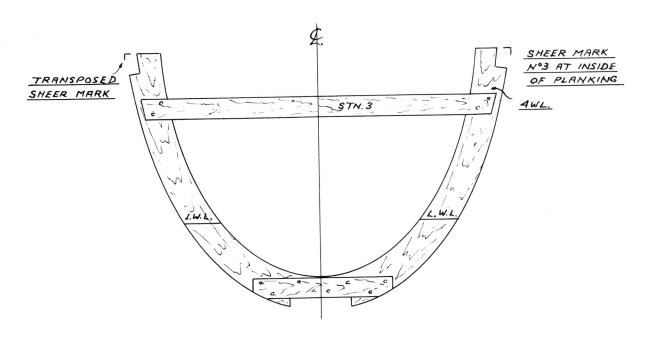

C̶L

SHEER MARK
N°3 AT INSIDE
OF PLANKING

TRANSPOSED
SHEER MARK

STN. 3

AWL.

L.W.L.

L.W.L.

COMPLETED MOULD

Fig 51

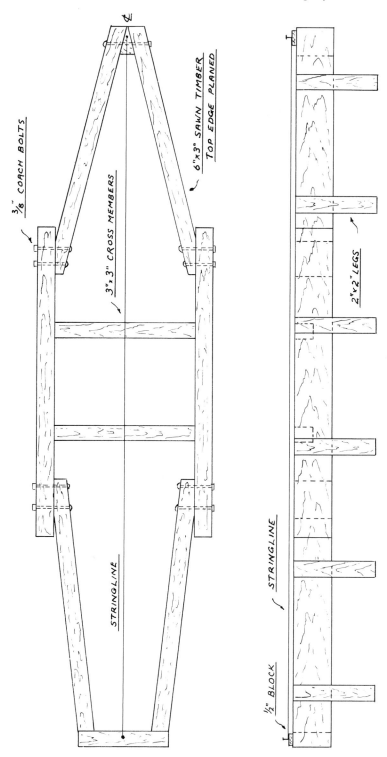

Fig 52 *Typical building stocks for setting up moulds*

89

The assembly of the two halves is done in the same manner as for the chine frames, with the sheer marks on the lofting being transposed to their opposite sides. Remember that it is the sheer mark at inside of the planking that needs to be transposed. The completed mould with gunwale and hog notches and spall is shown in Fig 51.

Building Stocks

The building stocks need to be substantial and completely rigid. The main frame can be 6 × 3ft softwood sawn. The top edges are best planed for clarity when marking out the station lines. A typical layout is shown in Figure 52, this configuration will be very much the same for most hulls. The whole must be set up level and square with the top edge about 12in above ground level. With the overlaps of the hull, this should allow access to the inside of the hull while planking up. The station lines are now drawn in on the top of the frame.

Because of the shape of the building frame, it is not accurate enough to measure the intervals along the non-parallel parts. To get over this problem, locate by approximate measurement station 5 on one side only. From this point mark in as many stations as you can on the parallel part of the frame. In the example it would be stations 3 to 8 inclusive. These station lines are now horned in on the opposite side by hooking a long tape over a nail at the forward end of the frame (Fig 53). As you can see in the Figure, a straight-edge is laid across at station 3 and using a square, the station interval is transferred to the edge of the frame. This is carried out on both sides. These station lines should also be checked by horning. As you proceed, so the straight-edge can be moved along. These lines are also squared down on the inner side of the frame.

Uprights of 2 × 2in can now be screwed or nailed to the inside of the frame. Stations 0 to 5 with their aft face on the station line at stations 6 to 10 with their forward face on the station line. At stations 0, 1, 2, 9 and 10, they should be bevelled to present a square face to the spall. To bring the correct face of the mould to the station line, a packing will be required on the posts, this being equal to the thickness of the mould material. These packing pieces can be fixed using Evo-stick™, quick and painless!

A string-line is now run down the centre of the frame and set on top of ½in blocks. These are used to maintain a datum level. It is inevitable that when erecting the moulds, the string-line will get kicked around and may well be displaced. If you have used cross members as in Figure 52, the line will be clear of all obstructions. The aft fixing of the string-line should be centred on the aft member of the frame. However if the frame is not square, then it is best to horn the position of the fixing from stations 7 or 8. In other words horning in reverse, by trial and error, as shown in Figure 53.

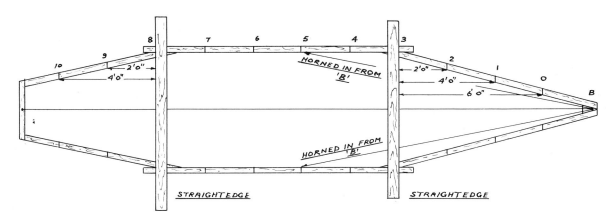

Fig 53 *Method of laying out stations*

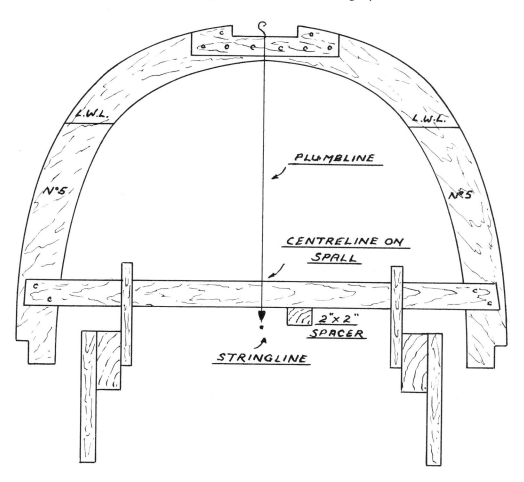

Fig 54 *Setting up a mould*

Setting up the Moulds

Setting up the moulds is best started at station 5, the cross spall being cramped to the posts as near central and about 2in above the string-line. A plumb-line is now dropped down as in Figure 54 (Do not forget to make a saw-cut in the hog notch for the line) to about ¼in above the string-line. Using the centre-line on the spall and the string-line, the mould can be levelled and centred. This can be time consuming single-handed so help is required. Having centred and levelled, cramp up. A 2in block can now be used to check the height of the spall above the string-line. The mould can now be adjusted up or down as

necessary. To aid this and to give a datum point for any adjustment, a line is drawn on both posts at top and bottom of the spall. The mould can now be adjusted so that the block just brushes the line, which should be as tight as possible. The mould can now be screwed to the posts and then positioned upright with either the plumb-line or a straight-edge and level, and securely braced. All the other moulds are dealt with in the same manner. It is a good plan to keep an eye on the LWL marks on both sides as work proceeds, so that any error in the setting up can be spotted at an early stage.

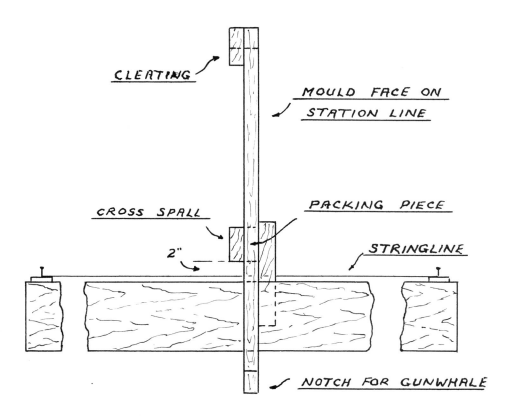

CLEATING

MOULD FACE ON
STATION LINE

CROSS SPALL

PACKING PIECE

STRINGLINE

2"

NOTCH FOR GUNWHALE

BUILDING FRAME

STN 1

CLEATING AT STATION 1

Fig 55 Setting up moulds

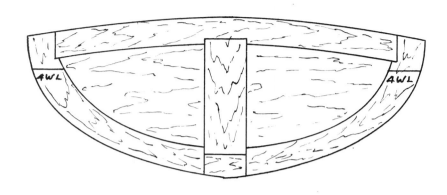

Fig 56 *Transom with framing*

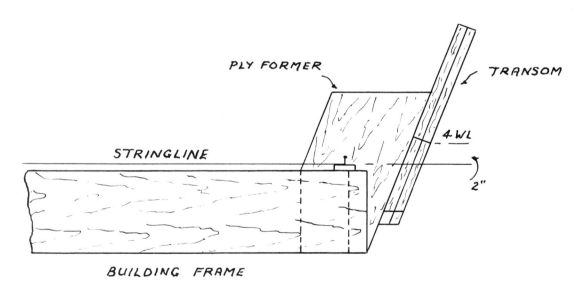

Fig 57 *Setting up the transom*

Transom

The transom is dealt with next. This must be traced off from the lofting, after the planking thickness has been subtracted. It should also have the deck crown added, together with a frame. If ply is chosen for the transom then this is quite straightforward; however if solid timber is to be used then perhaps two or three boards will need to be loose-tongued and glued up. The made-up transom will appear as in Figure 56 and set up as in Figure 57. It will be noted that the building fame should stop about 3in short of Station T1 to allow the transom to clear. The position of 4WL will be 2in above the string-line and can be levelled through with a spirit level and a 2½in block sitting on the frame. The transom is horned in to square it and should be well braced.

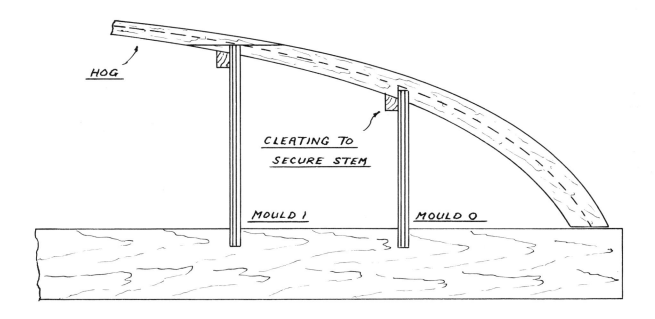

HOG

CLEATING TO
SECURE STEM

MOULD 1   MOULD 0

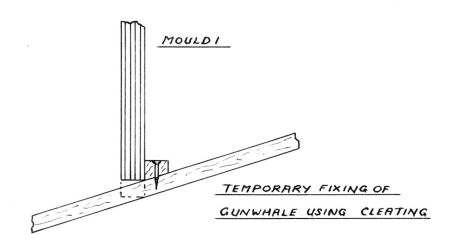

MOULD 1

TEMPORARY FIXING OF
GUNWHALE USING CLEATING

Fig 58 *Fitting the stem and hog*

Stem

The stem can either be sawn or laminated as described in Chapter 6. Note that the dotted line on the lofting is the face of the stem. Once the sides are cleaned up, the scarf can be put on and WL-BLW would be a convenient line for this at station 1. A centre-line should also be run down the face of the stem. The scarf angle is drawn in on the lofting and must be accurately cut. This will help later when laminating and fitting the hog. It is easier for the amateur at this stage to be able to offer the stem onto the moulds during the fairing, which is best done on the bench. Once you are nearly there, the stem can be set into place and secured with screws to blocks on the aft face as in Figure 58. A series of blocks must be fitted to all the moulds, and will be used to hold down the first lamination of the hog. It is wise to pre-drill the blocks, say two clearance holes in each.

Fairing

The whole structure can now be tried with fairing battens, particularly at stem and transom. If you have been careful with cutting out and setting up, there should be little fairing or adjustment to do.

Lastly, the gunwales are dry screwed from behind and let into the transom and stem. Blocks will be required to secure them as shown in Figure 58. Any errors found at this stage must be dealt with before planking starts, however minor they may appear.

Chapter 11

Round Bilge Strip Planking and Veneering

Strip planking and veneering are not difficult, the veneers only requiring a little shaping to one edge and the square-edge planking a slight bevel. The 'hollows and rounds' are the easiest and quickest to fit, with no further shaping to be done to them (Fig 59). Hand stapling the veneers, although not impossible, would be hard going as a certain amount of pressure is required to ensure good contact with the glue and under layers. Failure to do this will result in voids, and although not seen, can easily be found by tapping the veneer with a light hammer or better still a finger. If a void is found, a small hole is drilled in the veneer and glue injected with a syringe. Sometimes a void is caused by a natural 'bubble' in the veneer which cannot be pressed down. The answer here is to make several cuts with a knife, inject glue and re-staple. Be prepared! An icing syringe with a fine nozzle is ideal and is easy to clean with warm water. Getting back to the stapling, it may well be possible to borrow or hire a staple gun together with a small compressor. You will require a good supply of staples.

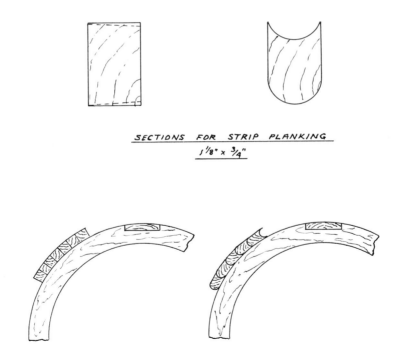

SECTIONS FOR STRIP PLANKING
1⅛" x ¾"

SQUARE EDGE SECTIONS
REQUIRE SLIGHT CHAMFER

"HOLLOWS AND ROUNDS"
LAY WELL AND CONTAIN
THE GLUE

Fig 59 *Typical strip planking sections*

Strip planking and veneers combine to make a strong, watertight and homogeneous hull and should present a nice easily faired and finished hull. Timber used for strip planking should be obtained in long lengths, straight grained and free from knots and shakes. Suitable timbers are mahogany, iroko, Douglas Fir, spruce or cedar. Veneers can be had in various thicknesses and widths up to about 12in, but for the purpose in hand 5 – 6in width is the easiest to handle. The type of timber normally used is either Agba or Kayha which are both mahogany. Kayha is the most popular and readily available. Veneers usually arrive in bundles containing a specified square footage or metreage. They will normally have sawn edges, so one edge should be shot by plane. While not in use lay them flat with a suitably weighted board on top.

Glues
The best glue to use for both strip planking and veneers is Cascophen Resorcinal Resin – 2 Part, as described in Chapter 5. As there are large areas to glue, the best method of application is a paint roller and tray. The roller and tray are easily washed using warm water. Another alternative is Epoxy Resin, using the appropriate formulation.

Hog and Stem
The hog lamination will need to be made up and scarfed. After cleaning up the scarfs, a centre-line and station lines are added and the widths marked in and faired in with a batten. As mentioned in the previous chapter, the stem scarf runs horizontally through station 1, so the hog laminations at this stage need to run about 6in past the station line and an inch or two beyond the transom.

The first lamination can now be cramped into position, having been cut back as near as possible to its finished length. This will provide greater accuracy when marking out. The method used is shown in Figure 60. After locating the back end of the scarf with a square, a line is now drawn parallel to the stem scarf. This is not strictly correct, however it is very close and easily corrected when offering into position. The second and subsequent laminations are dealt with in the same manner, by squaring down to the fore-edge of the

previous lamination. As each lamination is scarfed, the transom end can be cut to length. In the example, the transom end presents no problem as it meets the hog at little over a right angle.

The first lamination can now be screwed down from the underside at each mould, through the blocks and glued and screwed at the stem and into the transom frame. When using Resorcinal glue, any surplus should be washed off with warm water. The hog will need a considerable number of cramps, so ply cramps and wedges will be needed here.

Once the hog is complete it can be faired. This is best done by making a couple of saw-cuts at each mould and chopping out with a chisel as shown in Figure 61. A stiff batten is run over the moulds and against the hog and a line drawn along the side to represent the lower limit of the fairing. With laminations, this line can be confused with the glue lines so is best applied in colour. The bulk of the timber can be removed with an electric plane or chisel. When finally fairing, the fairing batten must be used diagonally over two or three moulds and carried on to the hog.

A flat is now planed onto the hog to provide an upstanding for the planking to butt onto, and provide a base for the keel. The flat in the example will run from station 6 to 12in forward of station 4 and should take the shape of the keel plate and will allow a 1in landing for the planking. A piece of timber, cut to the shape of the top of the keel and equal to the thickness of the planking is then laminated as in Figure 62. The profile of the pad can be drawn onto the hog before flattening. Great care must be taken to get this pad level in both directions. Before planking, narrow strips of polythene should be stapled to the moulds to prevent the planking sticking.

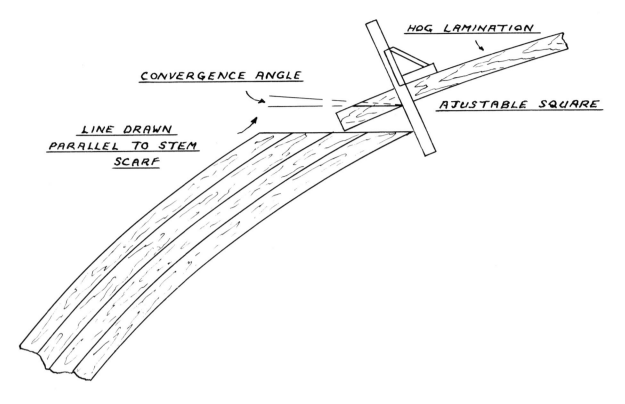

Fig 60 Scarfing hog at stem

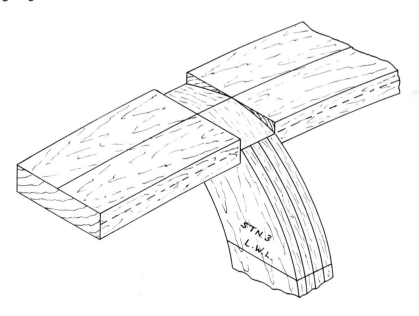

Fig 61 Wedges chiselled into the hog before fairing

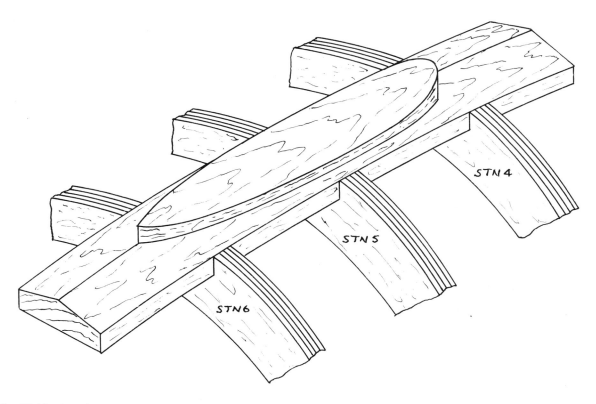

Fig 62 *Keel pad*

Planking

Planking is started at the gunwales. If hollows and rounds are being used, the hollow will be uppermost. The radius should be sawn or planed off the first plank, which is then glued and screwed to the gunwale, the bottom edge being left slightly proud, to leave a little to be faired off when it comes to decking. A plain butt-joint between lengths is quite satisfactory. Galvanised nails can be used throughout, with the planks being glued on-edge and to stem and transom. If using cedar, no pre-drilling for nails is required, but for iroko and mahogany it may be, depending on the hardness of the wood. To prevent damage to the hollow, the nails should only be set to the ridges and then punched in, although with a little practice, it can be done by tilting the hammer-head. It should be noted that all nail positions on the previous plank must be marked so as to avoid hitting their heads with the next row.

One very important point to watch for, whatever section you are using, but particularly with hollows and rounds, is to maintain close contact with the moulds. Sometimes it is not noticed for some time and then becomes almost impossible to correct because each plank locks into the previous one and so cannot be pulled in. If there is the slightest sign of this happening, the first thing to look for is fairness in the last one or two planks. If they show a slight deviation 'out' and we are only talking about 3mm, a block screwed on the nearest mould and a screw in the plank from behind will draw it back into place. If however the plank is fair, then there is more likely to be a flat on the mould which may have been missed when fairing-in. If this is found to be the case, the mould will have to be built up with veneer which only needs to be stapled on.

Planking should be secured evenly on both sides and the ends at the stem and transom sawn off as you proceed, but leave a little surplus to be planed flush later. A position will be reached, somewhere near the base of the stem, where the planking must be trimmed fore and aft, in other words it forms a mitre. This point is best determined in practice, as there is no predetermined position for this. The end-grain on the stem will eventually be capped after veneering and will merge into the hog. As the keel area is approached a few odd lengths may have to be introduced as it is highly unlikely that everything will go smoothly. The fore end of the keel seating, for instance, is an area that is radiused.

When the hull is completed all the minor ridges can be planed. The plane should be set fine and used diagonally. If the plane is used horizontally it will produce a series of flats that will prove difficult to remove. Now smooth the hull with an orbital sander or a Stikit 16in hand-file that are supplied by motor repair shops or chandlers. This is used in a similar style to a plane and produces a superb fair surface.

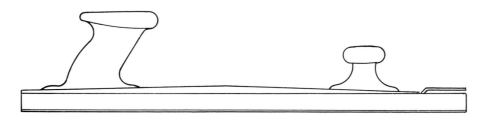

Fig 63 *3M Stikit Hand-file*

Veneers

Before starting on the veneers, it is sensible to prepare as many strips as possible. The best width is probably between 4in or 5in and they should have one planed edge. You should plan to make the most economical use of the material. If some of the veneers are 12in wide, then 2 × 6in is best. You will require one on each side with two planed edges. These are the first to be laid, one each side at or about station 5 and running aft at roughly 45° as shown in Figure 64. If the veneers are too short for this angle, then adjust to suit. Due to the upstand, the top end must be spiled. The veneers can be fitted up to the upstand, secured with a few staples and then smoothed down to the gunwale so that it takes its natural shape. This will become apparent when both edges lay flat and are in contact with the planking. The same principle must be applied to all veneers, and if you attempt to close the small gap caused by bad spiling by force, it may well lift one edge and thus become a problem to staple down correctly.

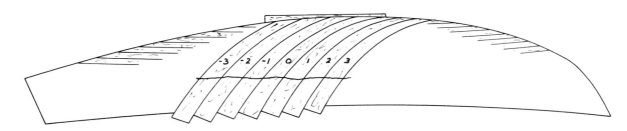

Fig 64 *Laying out veneer's numbering and pitch line*

Once the veneer is in place, it is held down by a few staples. A pencil line is now drawn down each side to clearly mark its position on the planking and each veneer strip clearly designated for position. Figure 65 illustrates a simple spiling tool. Working towards the stem, the next six or so must be spiled at the top edge. This should be done with the veneer as close as possible to the previous one and once spiled and trimmed, moved up tight to the keel and lightly stapled down. This can now be further spiled as shown in Figure 66. The greatest gap will determine which is the closest hole in the spiling tool that can be used, thus avoiding waste. This edge is now sawn and planed, the veneer offered up and stapled down at its top edge. The veneer is now progressively smoothed down checking the edge to edge fit as you go. A small shallow-angle plane is useful here for making any corrections required. If everything fits well, staple down. This procedure is pursued through to stem and transom. The veneers at the hog, stem and gunwales are best trimmed as you fit each one, although some folk leave it until they are glued.

Before removing the veneers, they must all be clearly numbered for relocation and a pencil line drawn across the face to help with alignment when glueing. Now you can glue and staple down, with particular attention to the edges. Having completed one side, the edge along the hog can be faired through to a clean fair line for the other side to butt on to. The first layer will require a little attention before the second layer is fitted. This second layer will run in the opposite direction and at roughly the same angle.

When removing the staples, some may break, leaving their legs inserted. This is not important on the first layer and difficult ones can be ignored. However on the second layer, circle them with a pencil and deal with them later. If any prove impossible to remove without damage, simply punch them in with a fine pin punch. Many a plane iron and spokeshave have been wounded by an embedded staple leg.

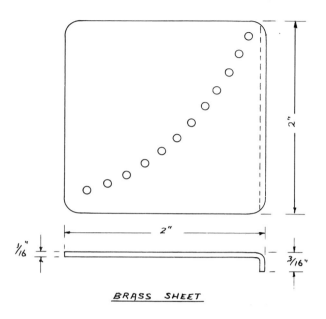

BRASS SHEET

Fig 65 *Spiling tool*

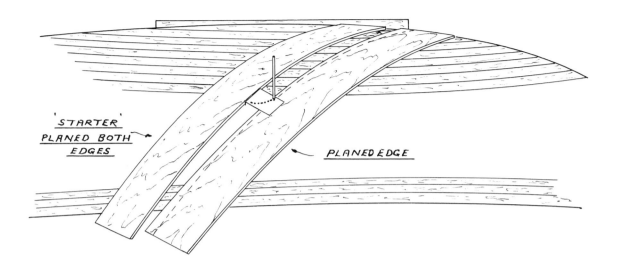

STARTER
PLANED BOTH
EDGES

PLANED EDGE

Fig 66 *Method of spiling veneers*

Turning the Hull

Before the final fairing of the hull, the remaining stem laminations should be screwed and glued into place. The hull can now be turned over, with lots of help, old tyres and mattresses. A suitable cradle can be made, using the body-plan for the shape as in Figure 67. The weight of the hull we have used as an example, at this stage weighs about 800lbs. Once turned, the hull must be levelled. This is simply achieved by reference to the cross spalls in both directions. Now most of the moulds can be removed, but leave numbers 2, 5 and 8. The inside of the hull, with its blobs and glue runs is cleaned with a fairly coarse disk sander. This is a very dirty and dusty task and suitable protective clothing should be worn, complete with face mask and goggles. Yes – it is that bad! Take care with the disk sander, especially with cedar which can be quite soft.

Floors and Bulkheads

Deck structures and accommodation have already been described in Chapters 8 and 9, but a short description here on floors and bulkheads will be useful.

The position of all bulkheads is marked on the gunwales, being horned in from the stem to ensure they are square to the centre-line of the hull. A length of 1 × 2in is set up on the marks and cramped into position. The plumb-line is then moved along the straight-edge and at 6in intervals dropped to the hull and tick marked as in Figure 68. The tick marks are then joined using a thin batten. You will find that this must be done in short lengths due to side distortion in a long batten.

An open template can be made up and to assist this, short blocks must be screwed to the hull to form a guide. There are several methods of fixing a bulkhead and the best is probably to glue and screw a frame around the bulkhead, allowing sufficient for a bevel. The frame will be made of short lengths sawn to shape. This should represent the thickness of the prepared internal framing. A second method is to secure the bulkhead firmly in place and run an epoxy fillet around on each side, and thirdly to fibreglass in with either polyester or epoxy resins. If this method is chosen, masking tape must be run around about 3in from the joint on both sides of the bulkhead to hull. This will help ensure a clean job. The tape is removed once the glassing is completed.

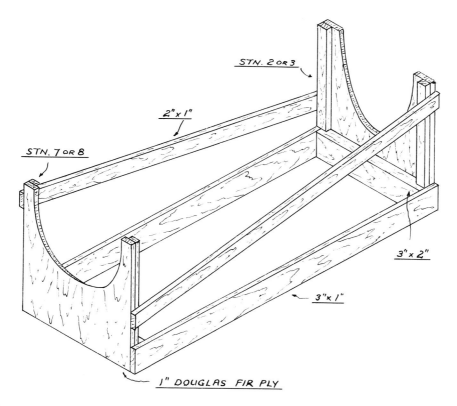

Fig 67 *Cradle for hull*

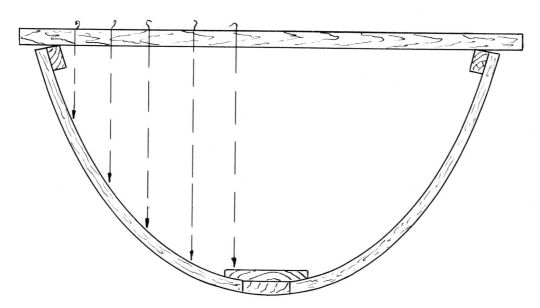

Fig 68 *Marking out a bulkhead using straight-edge and plumb-line*

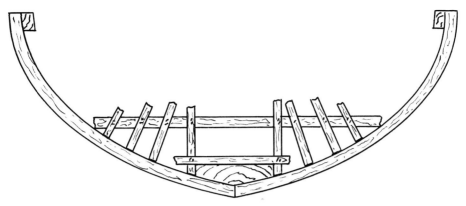

Fig 69 Making up a floor template

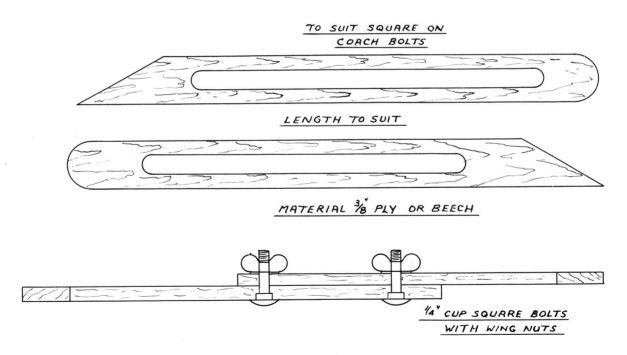

TO SUIT SQUARE ON
COACH BOLTS

LENGTH TO SUIT

MATERIAL ⅜" PLY OR BEECH

¼" CUP SQUARE BOLTS
WITH WING NUTS

Fig 70 Device for internal measurement and setting up floors

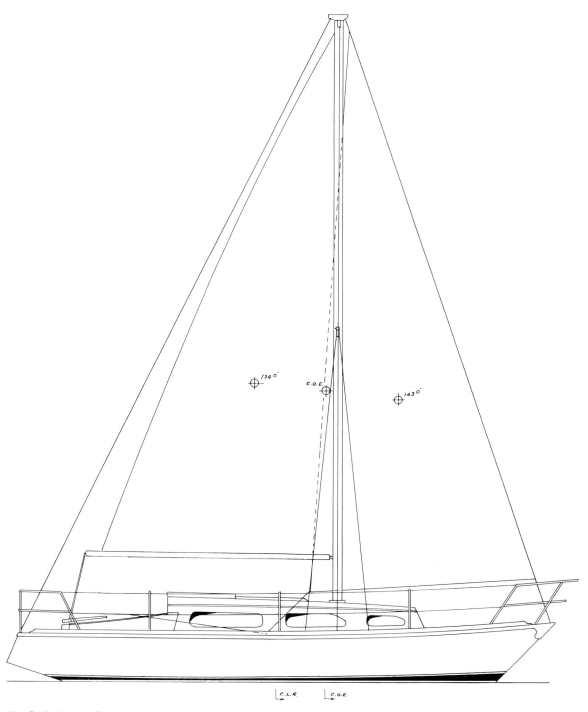

Fig 71 *Sailplan of Goosander 25*

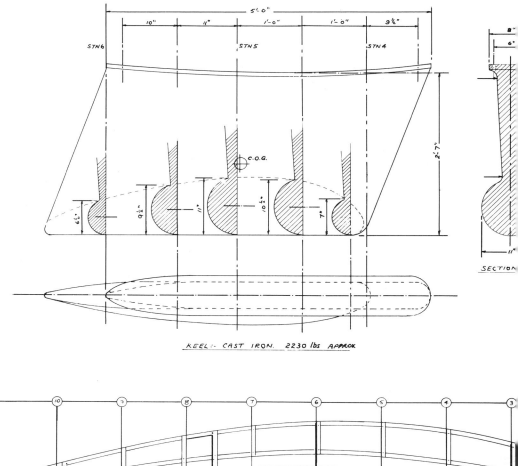

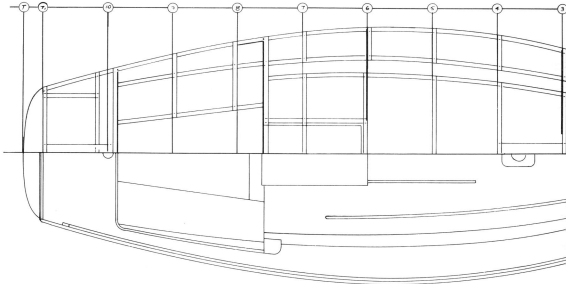

Fig 72 *Deck plan and keel details for Goosander 25*

	STN	B	O	1	2	3	4	5	6	7	8	9	10	T_1	T
HEIGHTS ABOVE AND BELOW L.W.L.	SHEER	2-11-0	2-6-6	2-5-5	2-4-2	2-3-2	2-2-6	2-2-5	2-2-6	2-3-0	2-3-1	2-3-2	2-3-2	2-3-3	
	BUT S						0-2-5	0-5-5	0-6-5	0-2-0	0-7-7				
	4				1-10-7	0-1-0	0-9-4	1-1-7	1-3-1	0-11-0	0-3-6	0-5-3			
	3			2-4-0	0-1-4	0-9-2	1-3-4	1-6-3	1-6-3	1-2-7	0-9-0	0-1-5	0-7-5	2-3-1	
	2			0-6-7	0-7-3	1-2-2	1-6-4	1-9-0	1-8-5	1-5-1	0-11-6	0-5-1	0-2-5	0-10-7	
	1		1-3-1	0-3-7	1-0-3	1-5-4	1-9-1	1-11-0	1-9-7	1-6-1	1-0-7	0-6-2	0-1-2	0-8-6	
	KEEL BOTTOM		0-0-0	0-3-4	1-3-3	1-6-5	1-10-5	2-0-0	1-10-6	1-7-1	1-1-6	0-7-2	0-0-0	0-8-0	0-10-5
HALF BREADTHS	SHEER	0-0-0	2-8-7	3-3-7	3-8-7	3-11-1	3-11-4	3-9-7	3-6-6	3-2-2	2-7-7	2-0-5			
	WL 4		0-11-4	1-10-4	2-7-7	3-3-5	3-8-7	3-11-1	3-11-4	3-9-7	3-6-5	3-1-5	2-7-1	1-11-6	
	3		0-8-7	1-8-4	2-6-6	3-3-0	3-8-5	3-11-1	3-11-4	3-9-7	3-6-3	3-0-7	2-6-1	1-10-3	
	2		0-6-2	1-6-3	2-4-6	3-1-3	3-7-2	3-10-2	3-10-3	3.8.6	3-5-2	2-11-4	2-3-2	1-5-0	
	1		0-3-4	1-3-5	2-2-3	2-11-2	3-5-4	3-8-7	3-9-1	3-7-3	3-3-4	2-8-4	1-9-1		
	L.W.L.		0-0-0	1-0-3	1-11-1	2-8-3	3-3-1	3-6-7	3-6-7	3-4-4	2-11-5	2-2-5	0-0-0		
	A.W.L.			0-7-8	1-7-2	2-4-7	3-0-4	3-5-1	3-5-4	3-2-2	2-7-3	1-6-4			
	B.W.L.			0-2-3	1-2-7	2-1-4	2-9-2	3-2-0	3-2-5	2-9-5	2-0-5				
	C.W.L				0-7-7	1-7-5	2-4-7	2-10-2	2-10-5	2-4-3	0-11-7				
	D.W.L.					0-11-7	1-10-1	2-3-7	2-4-7	1-7-7					
	E.W.L.						1-0-2	1-7-3	1-6-4						
DIAGS	A		0-8-3	1-7-2	2-4-6	3-0-5	3-7-1	3-10-3	3-10-6	3-7-3	3-2-5	2-8-4	1-11-4	1-2-7	1-0-3
	B		0-3-0	1-0-7	1-8-4	2-2-6	2-8-1	2-10-6	2-10-6	2-6-6	2-0-1	1-5-2	0-7-7		

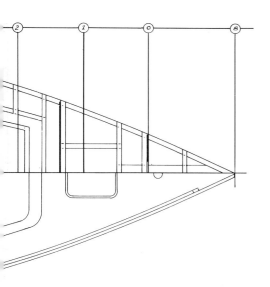

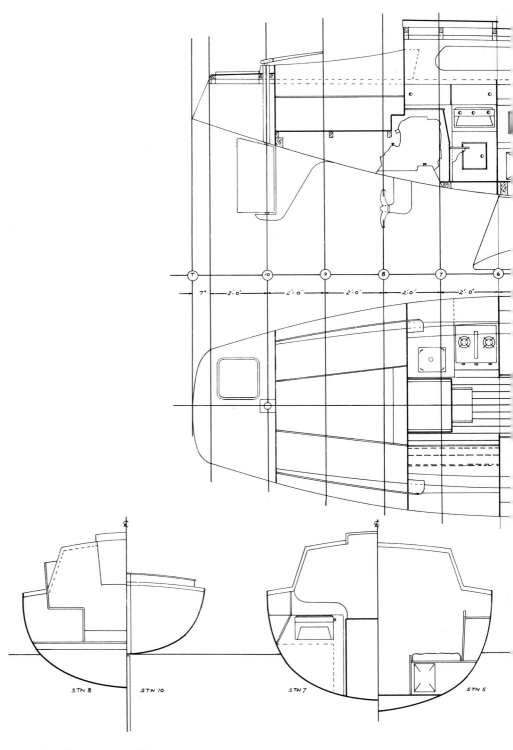

Fig 73 *Accommodation plan for Goosander 25*

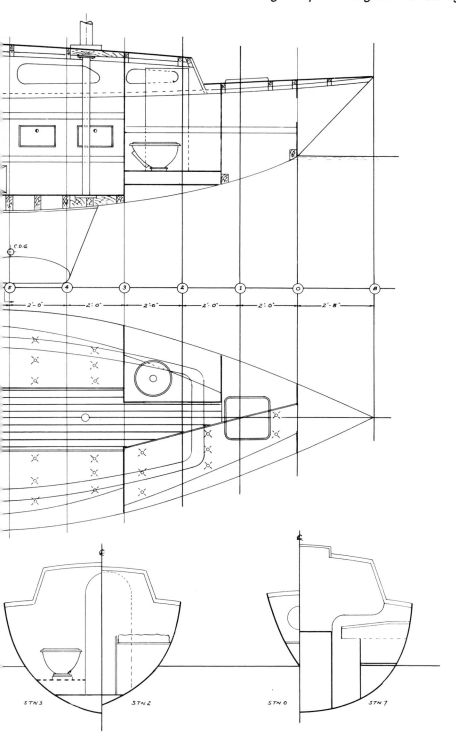

Skeg and Rudder

The two examples used in this book show two different types of rudder and methods of hanging. The chine-hull will be dealt with first. The rudder tube can be stainless, galvanised mild steel or GRP and fitted at both ends with a Delrin bearing which should be an interference-fit in the tube. The top end of the tube is located through a deck pad and the lower end taken through the horn timber and hog. In the case of stainless or mild steel tubes, a small plate can be welded to the lower end thus securing the tube firmly in place with plenty of mastic and the use of coach screws. If a GRP tube is used then the top and bottom ends need to protude about half an inch and be secured firmly in place with an epoxy fillet. Drilling for the rudder tube is not easy but it must be drilled accurately. As far as the '27' is concerned it is best done before the hull is planked, when the lower end can be drilled from inside and using a stringline as a guide. The '25' however will have to be drilled after planking and preferably before fitting the skeg. It is best to drill out the bottom end first and then insert a vertical straight-edge up to the deck pad and so locate the top end. Before having the rudder stock made it is best to measure the length required on the actual hull as opposed to the dimension that might be given on the drawing.

The skeg on the '25' can be fitted once the hull is the right way up and perfectly level. A suitable flat must be planed on the hull to conform with the top of the skeg. The skeg itself will need to be laminated from two pieces and fixed to the hull by glueing and using a long threaded rod running up through an additional floor. While making up the two halves of the skeg, a vertical slot can be cut into the inside faces to accommodate the rod and a 'window' cut through one piece to give access for fitting the end nut. One other excellent way of fixing is to extend the skeg in the form of a long narrow tongue through the hull and then bolt it to a bulkhead. This intrusion into the hull needs to be made watertight with mastic followed by an epoxy fillet at skeg and hull.

The rudders in both examples are made up of two laminations of ply. The '27' rudder being fitted with a pintle at the bottom which fits into a shoe bolted to the bottom of the sternpost. The top of the rudder stocks in both cases are best tapered and keyed to receive matching tiller heads. The rudder stock for the '25' differs from the '27' in as much that the tangs holding the rudder blade are internal. These tangs of which there are two should be welded to the stock at an angle of about twenty degrees and pointing upwards, eliminating the need for any fastenings. Both laminations will need slots cut in them to receive the tangs and also to be internally radiused at the fore end to blend in with the stock. This rudder is also fitted with a pintle and fits into a shoe at the base of the skeg. Both rudders should be tapered for about a third of their cord and radiused. All types of fittings will have to be made to suit.

Chapter 12

Finishing and Painting

There are three ways of finishing a boat. The first is by using conventional paint and varnish, the second by using a high performance scheme and the third by sheathing with glass cloth and epoxy resin, followed by a two-pot polyurethane finish.

There is a variety of products to choose from, so the following notes are intended as a general guide and the manufacturer's instructions should be followed closely.

Painting

Let us deal with the conventional paint finish first. Most people can paint and have done a fair bit on the house, however using enamel paint on a door at home is quite different to painting the large surface of a hull. It is generally accepted that success in painting is seventy-five per cent preparation. How boring you may say, but more often than not it is failure in that seventy-five per cent that spoils the finished result.

Everybody admires a well finished boat with gleaming paintwork and deep high-gloss varnish. There is no mystery how this appearance is achieved. It is simply careful and thorough preparation, quality paint, good brushes, the right weather conditions and not least, a certain degree of skill.

Results will depend very much on weather conditions, especially when the boat is finished in the open. Painting in extremes of weather will result in a poor finish. Most enamel paints are reasonably forgiving, but not so the two-pot polyurethanes. Conditions for that must be right before any attempt is made to use them. Any moisture in the air or in the timber will dull the finish and cause poor adhesion. Read the instructions carefully. These polyurethanes must not be applied over conventional paint or primer.

Apart from the weather, which should be warm and still, another problem is dust. This must be dealt with ruthlessly, particularly on the floor or ground in the vicinity of the hull. Sweep clean where possible, and dampen down when the dust has settled. It is also advisable not to wear woollen garments as these fibres tend to migrate onto brushes and painted surfaces.

Organise everything before you start applying the paint itself. The paint should be stirred well, the appropriate solvent close to hand along with lint-free rag, spare paintbrushes, tak rags and the trestles positioned. Painting with enamel paints means keeping the working edge wet and so the painting must be quick and continuous. Use the largest brush you can handle, with a smaller one ready to cover intricate areas. Lay-off with vertical strokes on vertical surfaces – this will minimise runs and curtains. Cheap, inferior brushes are out. The best quality brushes must be used to obtain a fine finish. Partially worn or stiff brushes can only be used for primer. Only load the brush to half bristle length. Brushes are expensive, so always clean them with the appropriate solvent and then wash them in soapy warm water when they are finished with. Dry them thoroughly and wrap in grease-proof paper in a fine chisel shape.

Returning to the boring bit, the hull must first be searched thoroughly and all holes, scratches and blemishes filled, smoothed and cleaned. This is best done with a sharp scraper and then sanded. The hull and deck are now sanded with an orbital sander, after which they should be sanded by hand in the direction of the grain. All dust is then removed, ideally with a vacuum cleaner and given a final wipe with a tak rag. Do not use turps or any kind of solvent as this will tend to raise the grain and therefore take you back to square one.

A coat of primer can now be applied and is normally thinned. Once this is thoroughly dry, rub down with 280 or 320 grade dry abrasive paper. This first coat of primer will reveal all those places that you thought were filled but weren't quite, so a further hull search for imperfections is required.

A word about filling seems appropriate here. Screw holes and deep indentations are almost impossible to fill completely in one go. As you press the filler in and drag the knife away, the filler tends to pull away from the edge of the hole. This can be rectified during the second application, so do not spend too much time attempting perfection on the first time round. The minimum of filler should be used, bearing in mind that any residue will need removing by scraping and sanding. It is quite a technique, but most folk soon get the hang of it and some even enjoy it.

Having completed the second round of filling, sanding and cleaning off, a second and third coat of primer is applied. This should now produce a good even application. At this stage the boot top should be masked off, as it will require special paint and the hull below it will be anti-fouled. The masking tape should never remain fixed for more than a day or two or it will tend to tear when removed or not wish to part with the hull at all. Scraping it off is difficult and leaves behind a film of adhesive on which solvents have little effect. Remove the tape soon after painting – remasking is a quick job.

When masking off, a similar method can be used to that adopted for positioning the waterline. Here, the tape is fixed to the stem and about half a boat length of tape unrolled and stretched away from the hull. It is then drawn in towards the hull until it gradually makes contact. An observer can help by indicating 'up or down'.You will be able to see if you have a straight line or if you must pull the tape off the hull and outwards to relocate it. Having reached maximum beam, expose a similar length and continue aft. The lengths nearest the stern and under the transom will need to be 'bent' round in short lengths. When all is well, the working edge can be pressed home securely with something like a chisel handle. It is possible to buy a 'Fine Line' tape, which is certainly effective but naturally more expensive.

The bottom can be left for now, but will need two coats of anti-fouling at a later stage. The keel must be wire brushed to obtain the cleanest possible surface and then dusted off. Apply five coats of metal primer, allowing the recommended drying times for each coat. The anti-fouling will follow.

At least two undercoats should be applied to the topsides, flatting in between. The object here is not only to produce a dense background for the topcoat but also to fill the grain and so produce a smooth surface. It is only when the glossy topcoat is applied that you will appreciate your efforts. After applying the first topcoat, it is advisable to rub down wet with wet or dry. If as a result you find there are shiny specks showing, it will mean that further coats are required. If the paintwork is brought up to a first-class finish at this stage, then any subsequent painting in the future will be that much easier.

Deck Paint

Non-slip deck paint containing sand is available in several colours. It can be effectively used to create a deck pattern in conjunction with a different shade of conventional paint around it. The deck will need filling and priming as for the hull. If intending to cover the entire deck with deck-paint, then apply two coats directly onto the primer. If creating a pattern, then the entire deck should be painted up to the topcoat and the required pattern drawn on and masked off with tape. Any radiused corners are left square and penciled in after masking. These areas should be abraded to provide a good key for the deck paint. The corners are rounded, freehand when painting.

If Treadmaster™ is to be used, the deck should be left bare. The required layout should be carefully designed and penciled on (Photos 12, & 13). The pattern must be identical on each side, except of course where there is something like a vent etc. Open templates are made directly over the penciled lines and then transferred to the Treadmaster for cutting out. Great care is required here to maintain the direction of the pattern, which should run fore and aft. To help maintain this, two tick marks, one at each end of the template are marked, representing the fore and aft line of the deck. These can then be aligned with the pattern of the Treadmaster. For marking out, a fine black felt-tip pen is most suitable, but stop short at the corners and create radiused corners with that ever useful tin. A sharp knife or large pair of scissors are best for cutting out.

Treadmaster supply an adhesive of their own or alternatively one can use an epoxy resin thickened with microfibres. This should be spread evenly on to the Treadmaster, which is then carefully positioned and stapled down ensuring

Photo 12 Coachroof and side-deck showing the layout of the Treadmaster

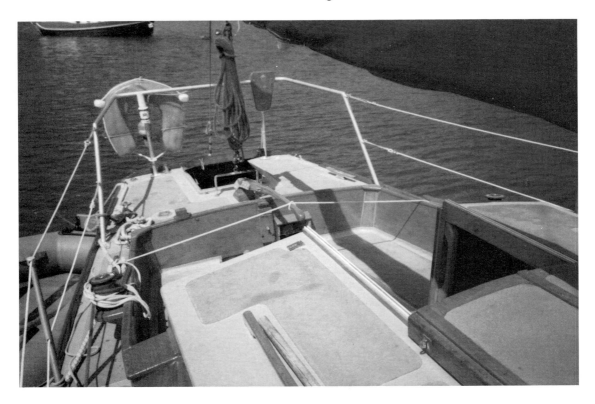

Photo 13 *Cockpit area showing Treadmaster and main hatch slides*

that no air remains trapped underneath. Stapling is best started in the middle and then working out to the edges, where great attention must given to the adhesion. Any surplus adhesive must be removed with a putty knife and any further residue with acetone. It is a good idea to use a block of wood and a hammer to ensure an even contact overall.

When using epoxy, only mix small quantities at a time as its usable life is rather short, especially in above average temperatures. One can cover two medium sized panels of Treadmaster at a time, working reasonably quickly.

The exposed deck between the Treadmaster can now be given two coats of primer, a minimum of two undercoats and two topcoats.

High Performance Paints

An alternative hull finish, called a high performance scheme, is based on a two-pot polyurethane paint and offers good waterproofing qualities and abrasion resistance. The initial surface preparation is as already described. For the topsides, apply a coat of clear primer followed by two undercoats, flatting down and followed by two topcoats. The same scheme is followed for the deck, with a non-slip additive in the final coat. The bottom up to the boot top, and the keel, are treated as described for the topsides. The scheme must have the right weather conditions for application and should not be attempted in any other conditions. Read the instructions with care. If you wish to use Treadmaster on the deck, it should be laid on a bare deck and the avenues treated as for topsides.

Varnishing

When varnishing, the timber requires careful preparation and all blemishes should be removed by either sanding or use of a cabinet scraper. Particular attention should be given to plugs making sure that they are flush with the surface. Hand sanding should be along the grain and all dust removed with a vacuum cleaner and finally a tak rag. Deal with dust as for painting and apply the same standards to your brushes. Varnish brushes are best kept in an equal mixture of turps and linseed oil. This will keep them supple and prevent specks of hardened varnish forming at the bristle base.

The first coat can either be a thinned coat of varnish or a clear primer. Clear primer dries fairly quickly and provides a hard smooth surface when rubbed down. When using clear primer do not use your best varnish brush but an older throw-away model and be sure to close the lid securely to stop it curing in the pot.

Now one can apply as many coats of varnish as required, flatting between each coat. It will probably need four or five coats before you see the results of your labours. The more you apply now, the fewer required in the future. The two most difficult timbers to varnish are teak and iroko because they contain oils. They must be degreased with acetone before varnishing; there are special varnishes produced for these woods.

There is a choice of gloss, matt or eggshell for interior varnish. The matt and eggshell need regular stirring to keep the dulling agent in suspension.

Solvents are expensive and with some products it is more economical to use disposable cheaper brushes, sold by most chandlers as laminating brushes.

Interior Painting
If the inside planking was not painted before fastening, it is best painted with a conventional finish. There are two ways of dealing with the bilge. Apply two coats of primer, followed by two coats of bilge paint or a superior finish would be to use two or three coats of epoxy resin composition. Take heed of the instructions regarding ventilation when using this and similar products.

Chapter 13
Sheathing with Epoxy Resin and Glass Cloth

Sheathing with epoxy and glass cloth not only adds to the strength of the hull, but also ensures watertight integrity. It will be assumed here that the deck is to be sheathed also. The deck and hull should be prepared as for painting and in addition the edge of the deck and corners of the transom will need to be suitably radiused. Glass does not like sharp corners.

A coat of epoxy resin can now be applied to the hull and deck, the resin being taken up all coamings to about ¾in. It is advisable to get a helper for this to keep you supplied with resin. The resin is best applied using a piece of thin flexible Formica or a plastic spreader about 4in wide and used like a squeegee, the epoxy being scooped out of the container with the spreader. Try to avoid runs or ridges because they are the devil to remove when the resin cures.

An epoxy fillet must now be run round hatches, cabin and cockpit coamings, as well as the garboard. Microballoons added to the resin make a good thixotropic paste. This should be thick enough to use easily but not slump. When it ceases to run off the fillet tool it is ready for use. When forming a fillet, first deposit as much as possible into the joint and then run the tool along, keeping it at right angles to the work. This should result in a smooth fillet. The excess on the tool should be scraped off and deposited further on. If the fillet is a little hollow in places or has a gap, a little resin can be added, but the whole length must be tooled again. You will find that a small quantity of resin escapes round the edge of the tool. This must be removed after completing a fillet and is best done with a pallet knife used flat.

Be careful not to disturb the feather edge of the fillet. As far as the corners are concerned, the tool should be carried round in one sweep and where a fillet is being carried on, the tooling should be started about 3in back, so as to obliterate any signs of a join.

The entire deck and hull should now be rubbed down and all runs and ridges removed. This is best tackled with a sharp scraper and the fillets with a short length of 1in dowel wrapped with 100 grit oxide paper. It's pretty tough stuff.

Glass Cloth

The cloth panels for the deck can now be cut to shape, remembering that there is no overlap at the vertical joins, but that they do have to run up to the top of the fillet and extend over the deck-edge by about 2in. A rough pencil guide is drawn on the deck to indicate the area to be covered by each piece. Great care must be taken to keep the cloth clean and free from any debris that may cling to it.

You will need a helper to mix and keep you supplied with the resin. It is advisable to use two containers for this and they should present a reasonable surface area as this will increase the usable time. Only sufficient resin should be mixed for one or two panels at a time, you will soon work out the optimum mix volume once you have laid a couple of panels. As in painting, everything must be organised before you start. A supply of disposable plastic gloves, spreaders, knife, scissors, acetone, a couple of brushes and a graduated mixing pot or mini pumps must be at hand.

Spread a film of resin on to one or two of the penciled areas and carefully place the cloth in position. The cloth must now be pressed down and smoothed out, with all wrinkles and air bubbles excluded. It is important to keep the joining edges as straight as possible. A further coat of resin is now applied and spread evenly over the cloth, with any excess being carried on to the next penciled area to be covered. The cloth should now become completely translucent. If however there are any white patches, more resin must be applied and stippled in with a stiffish brush. The fault here is usually insufficient resin being applied before the cloth was laid. If you

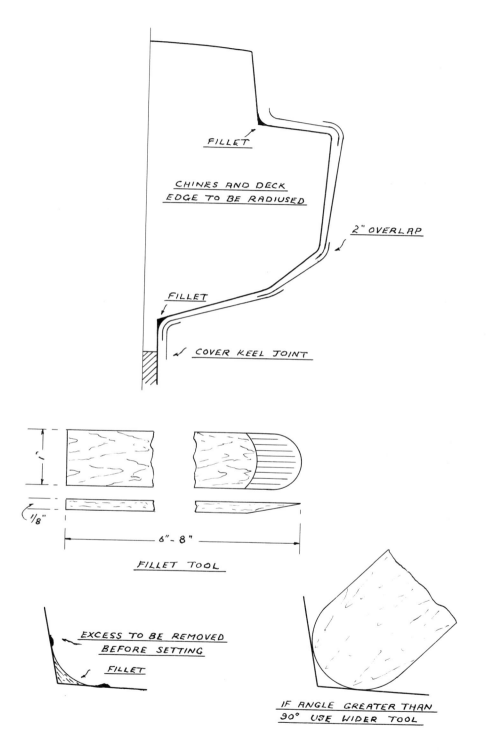

FILLET

CHINES AND DECK
EDGE TO BE RADIUSED

2" OVERLAP

FILLET

COVER KEEL JOINT

1/8"

6" - 8"

FILLET TOOL

EXCESS TO BE REMOVED
BEFORE SETTING

FILLET

IF ANGLE GREATER THAN
90° USE WIDER TOOL

Fig 74 Method of sheathing and fillet tool

overdo the resin, spread it on to the next area. Make sure that the edges are firmly down, especially where it runs over the deck-edge.

Smoothing the cloth down is best done with the hands. The cloth can be moved slightly and the weave will distort. This can be used to advantage when straightening out the joints. Where the cloth is tucked into a fillet it is best to stipple with a brush. If any trimming is required it can be done with a sharp knife – it is surprisingly easy at this stage. Have an old bucket or box ready for the offcuts. If the resin gets onto your clothes or shoes you have a problem. Acetone will help remove it if used quickly. Paper overalls can be bought quite cheaply and are a good investment. Some people are allergic to the resin, myself included, but I would add that it is only after prolonged exposure that the effects become uncomfortable.

Now to the topsides and a reference to Figure 74 will show the order of things. As described for the deck, the panels should be cut to length, that is from 2in over the deck to 2in below the top chine. The first panel at the stem will be triangular and wrap around the stem by an inch. To achieve an even overlap at the chine and deck, a 2in pencil margin can be drawn in. This will be quite visible beneath the cloth and will make for a neat finish when trimmed to the line. The limits of each panel are now penciled in. To help defy gravity when fixing these panels, they should be rolled onto a cardboard tube or length of large dowel. After sticking down the first two inches or so, the panel can be unrolled down the hull, smoothing out as you descend. Once it is in position the final coat of resin can be applied and as before, any excess resin applied to the next area. When approaching the transom, stop one

panel short and then do the transom, taking the cloth round onto the hull by an inch. The last hull panel must be trimmed to fit.

This is not always easy, so if an overlap is effected, a cut is made down the centre of the overlap and the two resulting offcuts removed and the new edges joined. The sheathing can be taken an inch or two over the keel where it joins the deadwood and this may prevent any potential leaks in this area.

Before packing up for the day, it is essential to remove surplus resin from the vertical edge of the last panel. This can be done with a scraper or chisel and will ensure that you have a good clearly defined edge to butt up to. You will find that when you are working the edges down, that an occasional thread will be picked up. This must be cut off at source. Do not try and disguise it by laying it down the edge or hoping that it will disappear, it won't. Any runs, blobs or ridges in the resin must be removed before the resin starts to gel. It is more difficult once the resin has cured.

The hull is now ready to be rubbed down. This is best done wet, attention being paid to feathering the overlap as much as possible without damaging the integrity of the cloth. On inspection it may be necessary to apply a further coat to the glass in some areas.

The hull and deck can now be finished with a high-performance paint scheme using two undercoats and two topcoats. Treadmaster can be laid and exposed deck treated for as hull. Below the boot top, the bottom should have three coats of epoxide resin composition, followed by two coats of anti-fouling. If the waterline and boot-top have been well scored in, they will be clearly visible beneath the cloth.

Chapter 14

Engine Installation

If building a chine-hull, the engine installation is more conveniently undertaken before planking. The first task is to bore the hole for the sterntube. This is a task that causes endless anxiety and that awful questioning of where it will reappear. I have carried out this operation several times, but I still suffer from the same trepidation and I guess it will never disappear. However, the job must be done – so here goes.

Sterntube

The boring can be done by using either a long twist-drill or an auger. I have used both methods and prefer the auger. Whichever you use, the centres should first be marked on the inboard shaft log. In our example this will be the face of the horn timber and the sternpost. These centres are squared-out and a batten stapled on the side of the deadwood as shown in Figure 75.

If you are to use an electric drill, a large morse bit, 1½in for our example, should be brazed onto a ¾in mild steel rod and then turned down to ½in at the end to accommodate the drill chuck. You will also require a ¾in bit for the initial pilot hole.

You must use a heavy duty and slow running drill. I have used one that became known as the 'gut buster' and this was fitted with two wing-handles upon which one hung on for dear life. Such a drill as this has little other use in the work-shop and is best hired.

Also to be hired, although probably for only a few beers, will be a helper whose task will be to keep you aligned to the batten, while you concentrate on keeping things square to amid-ships.

Start the pilot drilling by using the ¾in extended bit as slowly as possible, withdrawing every 2in to clear the hole of shavings. This will help you to run true. Eventually and hopefully you will exit in the right place.

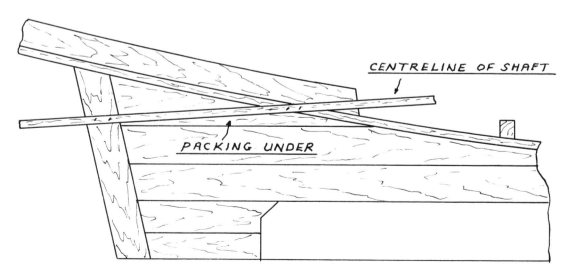

Fig 75 Guide for drilling the sterntube

Now we utilize our 1½in morse bit, which is pretty heavy and will need steadying support in the form of a wooden spar until it has entered about 2in and becomes self-supporting. Failure to keep things aligned at this early stage will result in an oval hole at emergence. Assuming that the pilot hole was accurate, then you should endeavour to keep an even shoulder as you proceed, using a torch to peer down the lengthening bore and adjusting your drilling angle to keep straight.

The choice of an auger means that no pilot hole can be drilled, since the tool is drawn into the wood by its own screw-cut point. An 18in or 24in hardwood handle will be required as the torque necessary to propel the device once it is biting is considerable. It will be slow progress,

withdrawing the auger periodically to clear the shavings and thread. This is essential to keep it pulling on down. Minor corrections to alignment can be made easily if made slowly and carefully.

Engine Bearers

If you have the engine or even detailed plans showing precise dimensions, the bearers can be made up and fitted. To do this, return to the lofting, draw in the height of the floors that will support the bearers, together with the line of the shaft. Now measure the undersides of the engine that are critical; the feet and drive coupling, making sure that you will have clearance for the sump and an oil tray when all is lined up with the shaft line (Fig 76).

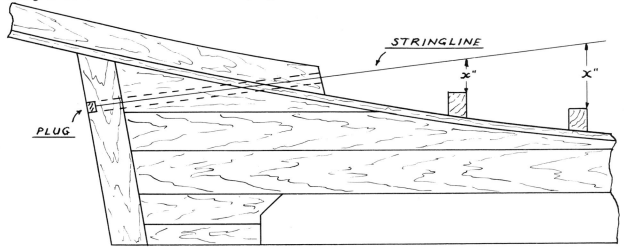

ACTUAL MEASUREMENTS TRANSFERRED TO LOFTING

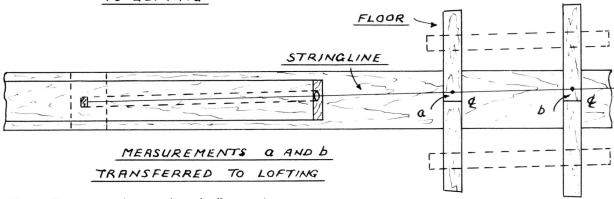

MEASUREMENTS *a* AND *b* TRANSFERRED TO LOFTING

Fig 76 *Exaggerated sterntube misalignment*

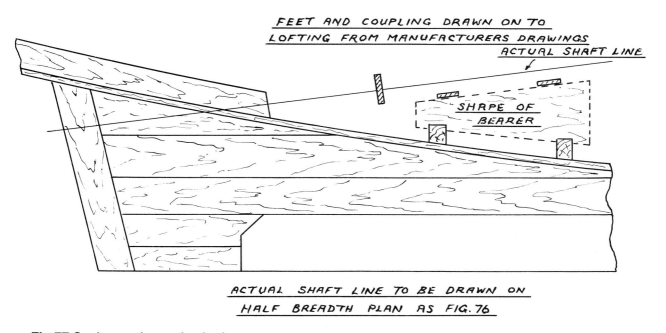

FEET AND COUPLING DRAWN ON TO
LOFTING FROM MANUFACTURERS DRAWINGS
ACTUAL SHAFT LINE

SHAPE OF BEARER

ACTUAL SHAFT LINE TO BE DRAWN ON
HALF BREADTH PLAN AS FIG. 76

Fig 77 *Setting up the engine beds*

If the sterntube bore proves to be slightly off centre, you can compensate by adopting the following procedure. Make up a wooden plug to fit the boring and drill a hole through its centre. Now pass a line through this hole and tie a stopper knot at the outer end so that you can thread the line up through the hole and pull the plug tight into the outer end of the bore. Now tighten the line from inside and make it fast to a cross bearer in the hull when you are happy that it represents the true angle of the drilled bore. By using the top of the aft floor as datum, measure up to the line vertically. This measurement is now transferred to the lofting and the resulting shaft line can be drawn in. The string-line can also be checked for any side error by using a vertical level down to the floors. If there is an error, then a point dropped to each floor will not only give the bearer centres but also the direction of their alignment as shown in Figure 76.

When you have the engine on its beds it can be worked aft to bring the couplings together. The beds should be arranged so that the engine mountings will have equal adjustment both up and down. There will be a slot in the baseplates to allow a certain amount of side adjustment.

The engine and shaft couplings can now be tested for alignment by inserting a three or four thousandth feeler gauge and running it through the coupling, noting where there is drag and where the feeler is slack. The forward end of the engine should be moved very slightly towards the side that is slack. Try again with the feeler until the drag is even all around the coupling. When satisfied, mark the engine feet with a fine sharp pencil to spot any movement and drill for the bolts. Insert them and tighten up. Check the coupling again and adjust if necessary until the fit is perfect. This will take some time but accuracy will pay dividends in the long run.

This is only a brief description and I would advise reading more technical books on engine mounting as the techniques vary according to the design of the boat concerned.

Chapter 15

Fitting Out

Now that the basic construction is complete and the boat painted and varnished, it is time to look at fitting-out.

Pushpit and Pulpit

Bolt down the feet to allow a space of at least ¾in to the toe-rail. This will allow access for deck painting between in the future and also means that when drilling down for the bolt holes that the hole is clear of the gunwale on the deckhead and leaves clearance for the nut to be applied. It will be now that you appreciate having applied the backing pads for deck fittings. You will find that almost every deck-fitting will require a below-deck helper to grasp the nut while you screw down from above.

If you intend to run the cables through the fittings to the navigation lights, now is the time to accommodate them. Personally, I prefer an external cable-run for ease of repair in case of failure. As with all deck-fittings, use plenty of mastic and watch where you walk! Machine screws are best suited for all deck-fittings and with the correct size hole are quickly inserted.

Fairleads

Certain fairleads for headsails and other running rigging are often positioned near the deck edge and these are normally screwed down. In most cases this will mean screwing through the deck and into the gunwale. Check the deckhead to see if a small pad will be required.

Stanchions

The pad drawing will give you positions for these. Stanchions must not lean outwards and should be vertical or preferably canted slightly inboard. Deck-top pads with a bevel will be required to angle them correctly. When making up these pads do not bring the inboard edge to a feather-edge. It should be at least ⅜in thick or it will tend to split when drilling for the fastenings and also when being tightened down.

Photo 14 *Foredeck showing pulpit and lifelines*

Thread the lifelines before fitting and remember that when using anodised aluminium stanchions and bases that is imperative to use the plastic sleeves provided for use in the bases, otherwise they may seize. As with the pushpit and pulpit, keep the bases inboard by about ¾in.

Sail Track

These must be bolted down well. The bolt holes will be at close centres so the tracks may need to be manoeuvred to avoid the fastenings fouling a bulkhead or running down the side of a deck beam. (If you have fitted Treadmaster, you should already have allowed for these fittings when planning the layout and cutting.)

Winches

When fitting winches, particularly onto or outside the cockpit coamings, attention must be paid to the running angle of the headsail sheets. There may be a slight change in this angle depending where the fairlead car is positioned, but if a turning block is used between the fairlead car and the winch, the problem is negated.

Filler Holes

Deck fillers for water and diesel are quite straightforward. It is good practice with larger holes through the deck to apply a little paint or better still epoxy resin to seal the cut through its thickness. Although mastic is used, this provides additional protection to the exposed ply or timber. Use a suitable hole cutter that will offer a good push fit.

Mast

The mast step will almost certainly require a wedge shaped pad to level it. It may also need a slight hollow on the underside so that it fits snugly onto the camber of the cabin top. For aesthetic reasons it is pleasing to have at least a 1in border showing clear of the mast step.

Electrical deck connectors for the masthead tricolour navigation light, deck spreader light and VHF antenna should be fitted as close as possible to the mast. You will need special connectors for VHF, GPS, Decca etc.

An alternative to buying a ready-made mast is the mast-kit. This can offer a considerable saving, but although they are relatively easy to assemble, the task takes more time than one might think. The particular kit that I have used was complete and included all fittings down to the plastic caps for the rivet heads. I hired a pop riveter from the manufacturer, and have in fact purchased it and found many uses for it since.

The assembly instructions were comprehensive and also included several useful tips, one of which was the method used for marking round the sections when cutting to length. Simply wrap a 2in wide piece of card round the section, line up

the overlap and pencil round. Now, simply hacksaw to the line. You will obviously need the correct size drills for the various holes, plus a round and a flat file. Lengths of light line are required to act as a pull-through (mouse) for the internal halyards. A small fishing weight is ideal to send it rattling down the section.

Chain Plates etc

The chain plates will have to be made up as detailed on the specialised fittings drawing supplied with your plans. They may be either stainless-steel or mild steel galvanised. In the examples here, they are specified galvanised mild steel, fully dimensioned with hole centres and the angles of the tangs shown. Suitable backing pads will have to be made up and in the case of the chine hull can be run from the underside of the shelf down to the top of the stringer, very similar to the butt straps and should be fitted once the hull is completed.

Make sure that when fitting cupboards or minor bulkheads that there are no obstructions to cause difficulty when finally fitting chain plates, which in both examples are fitted outside the hull and will be angled to the deck-line so as to provide a direct line to the rigging. These angles can be found by drawing the appropriate section of the sheer on the lofting boards, locating the position of the chain plates and erecting a vertical line from the centre one and striking a point equal to the height of the lower shrouds and then drawing in the rigging. These angles can now be transferred to the hull with a bevel. The chain plates must be well fastened, using penny washers under the nuts and be properly bedded with mastic. The rubbing strake can either be slotted out to accommodate the chain plates or better still, be fastened in sections by stopping short of the chain plates thus making their removal that much easier.

Down below, we can move on to complete the final phase of fitting-out. This of course will depend on the particular design you are building and the modifications that you wish to incorporate for yourself. Nevertheless some guidance on a few basic considerations should prove helpful here. One small but important item is the eyebolt that will secure the bitter end of the anchor cable. This should either be bolted through the chain locker bulkhead or screwed into the stem apron.

Heads

When fitting the marine toilet, carefully study the instructions relating to its relative level with the waterline and also the necessary height of the pipework. Faulty installation could cause syphoning and possible flooding. The toilet must be well secured on a substantial plinth. This is best approached by dry fitting the plinth, site and mark out the position of the toilet and drill for the machine screws. Countersink the underside of the plinth and push the machine screws up with a good coating of adhesive under the screw heads and then a further coat over them. Once these are set, the plinth can be screwed down dry, bearing in mind that at some time in the future you may wish to remove it for repair. The toilet can now be bolted down with nuts and washers. As stainless-steel nuts run freely there will be no undue strain on the screw heads.

The seacocks must be accessible for operation and also for maintenance. Reinforced flexible tubing is the most suitable for use with toilets. It is easy to cut with a hacksaw but can be difficult to get onto the spigots. (Immersion in hot water or hot air directed at that end should expand the tube sufficiently to slip it on.)

Water tank

These should be sited low down for obvious reasons and preferably near the centre of waterline length at about station 5. There are several types of tank available made in galvanised-steel, PVC, rubber or plastic. All but the plastic variety can be custom-made to suit the shape of the available space. I fitted two plastic ten gallon 'Aquaflow' tanks – one under each of the port and starboard berths between stations 4 and 5. These are interconnected under the cabin sole and the tank opposite the galley is vented to air. The deck filler is as in most cases 1½in and the remainder of the pipework is ½in plastic pipe. These particular tanks are not fitted with inspection covers, but after ten years of use I have experienced no problems at all. With a little ingenuity a clear plastic sight tube can be introduced into the system, which is connected to the vent pipe.

Cookers

Cookers, from a safety aspect, must be fitted with proper fiddle rails and pan-holders and

Photo 15 *Heads compartment. Note seacocks.*

should be fully gimbaled to allow for the boat's heel when sailing. There are many types powered by either gas, paraffin or alcohol. Gas is probably the most popular but important safety considerations are needed for its installation. Only approved piping should be used together with the recommended control valves. The location and storage of the gas bottles should be well away from the cooker and must be vented to the air. Since the gas used is heavier than air it will sink, so any storage box or compartment should be vented with a hole at the bottom and vented out to the side of the hull. Hang a gas bottle key in the locker, otherwise you will spend a lifetime searching for it around the boat.

Photo 16 Looking down into the cockpit of Goosander 27

Photo 17. Bilge pump situated in the cockpit

Batteries

Batteries, like water tanks, should be sited low down in the boat and also near the engine. Battery boxes should be strong and well secured, the height of the box being equal to the height of the battery. It is important to fit a retaining strap or other device to hold the battery down in the event of a knockdown. Airborne batteries will make a bad situation worse!

A master switch, with a changeover facility should be located for easy access. It will allow you to switch from one battery to the other or to run both for either usage or charging. When turned off it will isolate the batteries and prevent any leakage if the boat is left for long periods. With the advent of so much electrical equipment aboard boats, it is usual to have two batteries, one being dedicated to engine starting and the other for general use. I would suggest that the batteries be at least 75 amps each. Electrics and wiring are beyond the scope of this book but there are several books published dealing with all aspects of the subject.

Engine Box

If the engine box is to incorporate the companionway steps down into the cabin, as shown in Photos 5 and 10, then it will need to be substantial and located into cleating fixed to the bulkhead and retained in position with cabin hooks. Sound deadening material is well worthwhile, especially if fitting a diesel engine. Treadmaster fitted to the steps, and grab rails on each side are a great help in a seaway. Rubber strips of about ¼in thickness and 1in width can be glued to the aft and bottom edges to help deaden the noise and to form a seal against the bulkhead and sole. To fully utilize the space it is a good plan to build in a cave locker behind the top step for items needed to be grabbed from the cockpit in a hurry. As seen in the photograph mine is full!

Cockpit Drains

These should be at least 1½in diameter or better still 2in. The type of hose used for the toilet is the most suitable and connected to seacocks at the hull. Gate valves are quite suitable here and the hoses should be double clipped for extra safety. Crossing the pipes will help alleviate the problem of water surging up the leeward pipe when the boat is heeled.

Bilge Pump

The bilge pump is best located in the cockpit with the discharge carried out through the hull. The same 1½in hose is used here and led down along the inside of the hull to the lowest point of the bilge. As mentioned earlier, pre-drilled holes for pipe leads save a lot of hassle. Fit and screw a strum box to the hog. This is fitted with a filter and is easily cleaned. It can only take a small piece of debris, a matchstick for instance, to seriously effect the efficiency of the pump.

Fuel Tank

In a small boat, the only space left for the fuel tank is usually in the stern or cockpit locker. This could make it difficult to renew the filter or to drain the water-trap. Fuel tanks can be made of galvanised mild steel or stainless-steel. There are also rubber diesel fuel tanks which are specially reinforced, but cannot be used for petrol. Fuel lines should be copper with the last foot or so made of a suitable flexible pipe to absorb the engine vibration.

Photo 18 Goosander, *my own 27, taking to the water for the first time. It is moments like this that make it all worthwhile.*

Index